The Truth
about Kent State

The Truth about Kent State

A Challenge to the American Conscience

Peter Davies
and
The Board of
Church and Society of the
United Methodist Church

Farrar Straus Giroux
New York

Written for
ALLISON BETH KRAUSE

and dedicated to
SANDRA LEE SCHEUER
JEFFREY GLENN MILLER
WILLIAM K. SCHROEDER

Preface

In the fall of 1971, Dr. Cynthia Wedel, president of the National Council of Churches of Christ in the U.S.A., and Edwin Espy, the Council's general secretary, distributed a letter to the various denominational members of the Council. The substance of this letter was an appeal for contributions to make it financially possible for the litigation initiated by the families of those killed and wounded at Kent State University in Ohio and Jackson State College in Mississippi to be continued through the long process of appeals and counter-appeals. In a broader sense, the letter underscored why so many citizens are committed to this quest for justice. The following extracts from the Wedel-Espy letter serve to convey the extent of this commitment and the acute need for financial resources to sustain it:

> Someone has said that truth has become the fifth victim in the Kent State tragedy. Now that the Department of Justice will not use its great resources and its awesome powers for discovering the real truth about the shooting, the full responsibility has fallen upon the families and friends of those who were killed and wounded.
>
> The cost of continuing this pursuit of justice will be great, but the families have joined in committing themselves to searching out the truth and requiring the agencies of government to assume their responsibility under law. This will be done through private investigation and through cases presented to the courts at every level of appeal.
>
> In order to secure due process of law in the Kent State cases, the General Board of the National Council of Churches of Christ in the U.S.A. has authorized its Department of Social Justice to receive contributions in regard to the Kent State killings. "The Fund to Secure Due Process of Law: Kent State" will be used to receive tax-deductible contributions to assist in payment of the costs of investigation and litigation for the Kent State cases.
>
> Let us remember that for sixteen months the families of the victims used every possible channel of government through which to make their appeal for a judicial forum before which the facts of the case could be placed.

Although this fund will also assist the legal effort on behalf of the victims of the Jackson State shootings in May 1970, it has, unfortunately, had little support apart from the generous contribution by the Playboy Foundation. That effort in Mississippi has been spearheaded by Constance I. Slaughter, a dedicated attorney, and the Lawyers' Committee for Civil Rights Under Law. In Ohio, where suits were filed in federal and state courts, the legal battles have been led by Steven A. Sindell, a young Cleveland lawyer and, more recently, by Professor David E. Engdahl of Colorado University's Law School. These men and women continue to donate their knowledge and time to the struggle, but expenses for the preparation of lengthy briefs and for a widespread investigation which involves so many witnesses have already consumed many thousands of dollars.

Because of the continuing effort in Ohio, the Board of Church and Society of the United Methodist Church and I have donated half of all royalties accruing from the distribution and sale of this book to a special fund established by the Board as a repository for these royalties. This special fund has been set up to ensure disbursement of the receipts to attorneys in Ohio who represent the families of those killed and wounded at Kent State University. The other half of the royalties will be divided equally between the Board's Department of Law, Justice and Community Relations and myself, toward offsetting past and future expenditures in a quest for justice in the Kent State killings that does not cease with the publication of this book. We hope that the book will generate renewed support for the Kent State and Jackson State Fund to Secure Due Process of Law at the National Council of Churches, 475 Riverside Drive, New York, N.Y.

We express this hope because we are convinced that only through our courts of law, or perhaps a Congressional investigation, can the answers to so many questions be forthcoming, even the haunting questions of a bewildered mother. Three years ago, when the first shots rang out across the campus of Kent State University, her daughter sought the protection of a parked car. The young woman student was 343 feet from the National Guardsmen who were shooting, but she didn't make it. Her last words to the young man grasping her hand were simply: "I'm hit." A year later the mother asked some questions, not only for her dead daughter and for those who died with her, but for all victims of injustice: "She was only with us for nineteen years. And when we go to her grave tomorrow, what do we say? Do we say that there is no justice, Allison? No one cares that you're dead, Allison? That you were —executed? Or do we say there is justice, Allison?"

P.D.

Contents

With so many unanswered questions surrounding the four murders at Kent State to burden the American conscience, I find it almost incomprehensible that the U.S. Attorney General could close the official books on the May 4th tragedy while paradoxically agreeing with previous investigations that the shooting deaths were "unnecessary, unwarranted and inexcusable."

Ohio National Guardsman
Akron *Beacon Journal*
August 17, 1971

Sandra Scheuer   William Schroeder

Jeffrey Miller   Allison Krause

Introduction

We must look to the university that receives our children. Is it prepared to deal with the challenge of the non-democratic left? One modest suggestion for my friends in the academic community: the next time a mob of students, waving their non-negotiable demands, starts pitching bricks and rocks at the Student Union—just imagine they are wearing brown shirts or white sheets and act accordingly.

Vice President
Spiro Agnew
April 1970

At the peak of the 1968 Presidential campaign, Richard Nixon told the electorate that the country was torn by division though it wanted unity. "America has suffered from a fever of words," he said, "from inflated rhetoric that promises more than it can deliver; from angry rhetoric that fans discontent into hatred; from bombastic rhetoric that postures instead of persuading. We cannot learn from one another until we stop shouting at one another—until we speak quietly enough so that our words can be heard as well as our voices."

In less than two years the victors of that election had become masterful exponents of inflated, angry, bombastic rhetoric and evinced little inclination to learn from the dissenting opinions of others. Vice President Agnew fanned discontent into hatred with his infatuation for unusual adjectives, so the divisions of the late sixties were aggravated rather than healed. In the spring of 1970 the war in Southeast Asia seemed to be winding down, and for student activists, protest and concern focused more on the domestic problems of poverty, pollution, and racial discrimination than on events in the Far East. This situation changed dramatically on the night of April 30, 1970, when President Nixon announced his decision to support the South Vietnamese invasion of Cambodia with American ground troops.

Reaction on many campuses was immediate, but few people, myself included, were aware of the disturbance taking place on the campus of the generally conservative Kent State University in Ohio. It was during this final week of April that Vice President Agnew spoke in Florida at a Republican fund-raising dinner and recommended that violent dissenters on our campuses be treated as if they were Nazis. At week's end President Nixon spoke at the Pentagon and categorized such students as "bums." This crude characterization did not attract any great attention until a few days later, when the eyes of the world were distracted from the war in Cambodia by a thirteen-second volley of gunfire in Ohio.

Now it appears that what was initially reported to be wild, indiscriminate shooting on the part of some thirty ill-trained and frightened young Ohio National Guardsmen may well have been a premeditated barrage by about ten experienced, riot-trained guardsmen, with the remaining troops firing in reaction. The gunfire claimed the lives of four students hundreds of feet away. They died as the result of an explosion of emotions incited by exactly the kind of rhetoric on the part of Ohio's political and military leaders which President Nixon had found so undesirable during his campaign for election. Nine other students were wounded. One was paralyzed and another maimed. It was an event of tragic proportion, but what happened afterward is the real tragedy of Kent State.

Before the news media had reported more than the bare facts, Americans were voicing approval of the guardsmen's actions, or unquestioningly accepting it as the inevitable consequence of violent dissent. They were encouraged by a shaken Ohio general who claimed that his men had faced serious injury, if not death, and by the President of the United States, who, although as uninformed as the rest of us, issued a statement to the effect that when dissent turns to violence it invites tragedy. In other words, the kids asked for it. This comment not only set the tone for public opinion but precluded the President's reversing himself when it became apparent that the violence on May 4, 1970, had in fact been perpetrated by a few members of the Ohio National Guard. Justice could not be done, because President Nixon had implied that the shooting was justified, and the people generally agreed with him.

Ironically, Vice President Agnew disagreed. Three days after the shooting, the Vice President appeared on television in an interview with David Frost. During their conversation the following exchange took place:

DAVID FROST: But you think that the guardsmen obviously went far too far?

VICE PRESIDENT: Oh, yes, there is no question about that.

DAVID FROST: What if it is discovered there was no shot fired at them by a sniper and they just opened fire without a warning shot or anything? Not having been fired at in any way, in that sense what is the word for that, murder?

VICE PRESIDENT: Yes, but not first degree. As a lawyer, I am conversant, and I suppose most people who follow the courts are conversant, with the fact that where there is no premeditation but simply an over-response in the heat of anger that results in a killing, it's murder. It's not premeditated, but it's a murder, and certainly can't be condoned.

This was the last truly candid public statement regarding the shootings at Kent State by a member of the Nixon Administration, which grew

3

more reticent as a whole when subsequent investigations, especially that by the FBI, confirmed that the guardsmen had not been fired at by a sniper, that they had turned on the students and started shooting without any warning whatever.

Within twenty-four hours of the killings, Ohio authorities had painted a lurid picture of anarchy, the guardsmen portrayed as terrified kids with their backs to the wall, reluctantly shooting at a charging mob of hard-core revolutionaries. That night, the adjutant general of the Ohio National Guard, Sylvester Del Corso, was heard on a radio talk show in Cleveland. As reported by Eszterhas and Roberts, the general assured the program host, Alan Douglas, that his men had been fired at by a sniper from the roof of a building off campus. When Douglas pointed out the distance from buildings on city property to the Commons, and the fact that those buildings are only two stories high, Del Corso became somewhat flustered. The next day Del Corso told one reporter that there had been no sniper, and only a few hours later reversed himself while talking with another reporter and once again maintained that a sniper had been present. Once again the great American phantom sniper was invoked as an excuse for the shooting, but this time the claim was swiftly discredited by the Ohio State Highway Patrol and later by the Justice Department. Yet many people still believe Del Corso, and at the time this explanation fitted in with the preconceived notions of the majority, who, following the President's lead, had jumped to erroneous conclusions. The National Guard would never shoot at unarmed civilians except as a necessary and last resort. This assumption remains fixed in the minds of many Americans today despite all the evidence to the contrary which has come to light in official and unofficial investigations. Public outrage remains minimal and the Nixon Administration's silence politically tenable.

Three days after the shooting, enough had been reported in the press to convince a few people that the arbitrary condemnation of the students was not only unfounded but posed a grave threat to the initiation of an impartial judicial inquiry. The Nixon Administration had demonstrated its willingness to use the Justice Department as a political weapon against dissenters, and I was alarmed by the attitude of so many of my friends toward this crime. "It's too bad, but they got what they deserved" was the most prevalent reaction, when all I was able to think was that any one of the dead might have been my child.

On May 8, 1970, I wrote a letter to President Nixon expressing my concern, and my hope that he would recognize that such unwarranted force was inexcusable. I did not realize then that this letter would transform my life, a change that began several days later when I sent a copy of the letter to the parents of Allison Krause, one of the two young women killed by the guardsmen. I hoped that my words to President Nixon might bring them some comfort.

I communicated my sorrow to the Krauses because I had mentioned their daughter in my letter to President Nixon. "The full horror of what has happened in Ohio," I wrote, "is surely revealed in a simple act which we cannot and must not forget." That act was Allison's placing a flower in the rifle of a guardsman and saying, "Flowers are better than bullets." Later we learned that she had not done this but had said those words, to a National Guard officer—words that will forever be her legacy.

On Wednesday, May 13, Arthur Krause called me from Pittsburgh to express his appreciation for my letter to the President. This gesture on his part sealed my commitment to ensure that justice was done in this cruel and senseless act. Eleven days later, the Akron *Beacon Journal,* along with other papers in the Knight Newspapers chain, published a special 30,000-word report on what had happened at Kent State and why. It was investigative journalism of a high order and would bring the *Beacon Journal* a Pulitzer Prize. The Knight team found that some guardsmen had deliberately aimed at students and that in firing they had "violated regulations which stress 'restraint' and 'minimum application of force.' " The team charged Brigadier General Robert H. Canterbury, the senior Ohio National Guard officer at the scene of the shooting, with exercising "no control over the men on the hill under his command"—the men who eventually fired.

In July of that year, the same newspaper published a copyrighted story revealing the contents of a Justice Department eight-page summary of the FBI investigation which had started the day after the killings and at one point involved more than three hundred agents. The principal conclusions reached in the Justice Department memorandum confirmed our own feelings about May 4:

1. The shooting was not necessary and was not in order.
2. There was no sniper.
3. The guardsmen were not surrounded.
4. The Guard still had tear gas available when some of the men resorted to gunfire.
5. Contrary to claims by the Ohio National Guard, only a few guardsmen had been injured and only one sufficiently to warrant any kind of medical treatment.
6. At the time of the shooting, no student posed a threat to the lives of the guardsmen.

There was, in other words, no excuse for the shooting and, at this stage, Attorney General John Mitchell conceded that there were probable violations of federal law by some students and by some Ohio National Guardsmen.

5

In the aftermath of the killing of two Jackson State College students on May 14, 1970, just ten days after the Kent State shootings, President Nixon convened a special commission. In both the Kent State and the Jackson incidents there were charges of official violence, and the commission's task was to investigate the shootings and campus unrest generally. William Scranton, former Republican governor of Pennsylvania, was chosen to be the commission's chairman.

Thereafter, Ohio Governor James A. Rhodes announced the convening of a special grand jury to investigate Kent State. This effectively blocked any action by a federal grand jury for the time being and provided Ohio political and military leaders with a forum in which to cleanse themselves of any responsibility for the killing and wounding of the thirteen students.

In September, at the Ravenna courthouse in Portage County, the grand jury started taking testimony in secret, and though newsmen were barred even from the building, it was painfully clear to most observers that the grand jury would condone the actions of the Ohio National Guard.

In a prelude to the Ohio grand jury's predictable conclusions, the Scranton Commission released its findings. The shooting at Kent State, the commission concluded, "was unnecessary, unwarranted and inexcusable." The gunfire at Jackson State, the commission also stated, was "an unreasonable, unjustified over-reaction." The path was now cleared for Mitchell to convene a federal grand jury to investigate Kent State, as he had done for Jackson State. His own department and President Nixon's commission had reached the same conclusion: the killings at Kent State were "inexcusable." On October 16, however, the Ohio grand jury placed the blame on the students and on the university administration for permitting the incident to occur. As for the National Guard, they had fired "in the honest and sincere belief" that, had they not done so, they would have suffered bodily injury and possibly death. Not only did this conclusion fly in the face of the FBI report and the President's commission, but the photographs contained in the commission's special section on Kent State gave the lie to this statement by the grand jury.

At the end of October, *The New York Times* published excerpts from a second, and much more detailed, thirty-five-page Justice Department summary of the massive FBI investigation. The principal conclusions of the earlier summary were reiterated, but in the new memorandum much more serious charges were leveled against the Ohio National Guard:

1. The Justice Department had some reason to believe that, subsequent to the shooting, guardsmen had conspired to fabricate their story of self-defense.

6

2. Of those guardsmen who had not admitted shooting, the Justice Department believed that two, and possibly more, had lied to federal agents—in itself a criminal offense.
3. From statements given to FBI agents, it was established that Sergeant Lawrence Shafer of Troop G had deliberately aimed at and shot student Joseph Lewis, who had been standing sixty feet from the firing line. Lewis had thrown nothing at the guardsmen. He had taunted them with an upraised finger. Lewis was maimed.
4. The Justice Department could find no explanation for the shooting, aside from "any questions of specific intent on the part of the Guardsmen or a predisposition to use their weapons."

It now appeared that the facts were in accord with Vice President Agnew's definition of second-degree murder or manslaughter. But the questions why and by whom remained.

In December, Joseph Rhodes, Jr., a member of the Scranton Commission, said that two guardsmen had gone to Kent State with the intent to shoot at students and that the FBI knew who they were. But the year 1970 ended without a word from Mitchell about what action he intended to take in light of his own department's allegations against the Ohio National Guard and the commission's condemnation of the shooting. By now, most of the families of the dead and wounded had filed suits against Governor Rhodes, the generals, Kent State President Robert I. White, and individual guardsmen. In federal court these suits claimed violations of the young people's civil rights; in state court the litigation alleged wrongful death and injury. Arthur Krause also filed suit against the state of Ohio, an almost futile action in the light of Ohio's archaic doctrine of sovereign immunity. "The king can do no wrong" is how Krause described it, and the label is accurate. This throwback to the Middle Ages is totally incompatible with the spirit of our Constitution, but time and time again it has been sustained by Ohio's Supreme Court and ignored by Ohio's legislature.

Inevitably, these suits aroused indignation, and the parents of the young people received considerable hate mail accusing them of seeking to make money from the shedding of their children's blood. Nothing could be less true. At the very least, there had been negligence, and it was becoming more and more obvious that justice in this case was going to be circumvented, mocked, undermined. The families had two options: accept the idea that the young people had been unjustly killed and live with that, or seek the truth about May 4 in the forum our country provides for impartial and equitable assessment of responsibility: the courtroom.

In March 1971 the Reverend John P. Adams joined our quest for justice. He called Arthur Krause after reading in the Washington *Post* that Mitchell planned to close his file on Kent State. In his capacity as director of the Department of Law, Justice and Community Relations of the United Methodist Church's Board of Church and Society, Adams had been working closely with those involved in trying to secure justice in the Jackson State killings. Adams was able to arrange for a meeting with Jerris Leonard, who was at that time head of the Justice Department's Civil Rights Division. More meetings followed, and in May, two weeks after the first anniversary of the killings at Kent State, Adams and attorney Steven Sindell met with Richard Kleindienst, then Deputy Attorney General.

The meeting with Kleindienst was prompted by the belief that Leonard's successor, David Norman, had already submitted his recommendation on the convening of a federal grand jury to Mitchell. Not so, Kleindienst told Adams and Sindell. The matter was still under consideration, and if they had a constructive case to present for review, they should meet with Norman. The shooting, it seemed to Sindell, violated Section 242 of the United States Code, Title 18, dealing with individuals' civil rights, but there were strong indications in both photographs and the testimony of witnesses before the Scranton Commission that the shooting may very well have resulted from what the Justice Department itself called "specific intent" and that therefore some of the guardsmen may also have violated Section 241 of the same code. This section provides penalties for "two or more persons" who "conspire to injure, oppress, threaten or intimidate any citizen in the free exercise or enjoyment of any right or privilege secured to him by the Constitution or laws of the United States." Had some guardsmen gotten together just minutes before the shooting and decided among themselves that upon a signal they would fire at the students who had been harassing them ever since they started out to disperse the noon rally of May 4? The shooting took place twenty-four minutes after the guardsmen first moved out to break up the rally. This was the question put to Kleindienst, and, surprisingly, he did not dismiss it out of hand. On the contrary, he told Adams and Sindell that the Civil Rights Division had not even considered this possibility. Adams indicated that we believed there was compelling evidence that a decision had been made beforehand to shoot. The Deputy Attorney General assured Adams that the department would consider whatever evidence we had to offer, and he suggested that we submit it in a "substantive" format to David Norman. In fact, Kleindienst arranged the meeting with Norman.

That day, May 17, I began preparation of the argument for a federal grand jury to investigate a possible violation of Section 241 of the U.S. Code. In a month I put together a 227-page report which included some seventy photographs taken on May 4. This report argued that just the possibility of premeditation warranted federal investigation. The

Board of Church and Society brought out my report in a limited edition of ninety copies and, on June 21, 1971, it was submitted to David Norman. The next day, copies were presented to the offices of Mitchell and Kleindienst, to William Scranton and other members of the President's commission. Later, copies were sent to officials in Ohio, including the Attorney General and the Portage County Prosecutor. The thrust of the argument was the possibility that some guardsmen had conspired to shoot at the students. This possibility was suggested by James A. Michener, whose massive book *Kent State: What Happened and Why* was published at the end of April. "It seems likely," Michener said, "that some kind of rough verbal agreement had been reached among the troops." Whether or not this is what actually happened was clearly something only a federal grand jury or congressional investigation could determine.

By July 22 we had heard nothing from Norman, not even an acknowledgment that our *Appeal for Justice* was under review, so Reverend Adams decided to release the report to the public. On August 13, Attorney General Mitchell announced his decision, and we realized that Kleindienst had, wittingly or unwittingly, lured us into providing the Justice Department with the line of argument by which it could justify its refusal to convene a federal jury and at the same time neatly sidestep the violation of the students' civil rights under Section 242 of the U.S. Code. Mitchell conceded that the shooting was "unnecessary, unwarranted and inexcusable," but there was nothing the Justice Department could do about it since there was "no credible evidence of a conspiracy between National Guardsmen to shoot students on the campus . . . and no likelihood of successful prosecution of individual guardsmen." With those words the trap into which Adams and I had been led was sprung. Mitchell's statement contained no mention whatever of Section 242, the law the Justice Department summary had intimated six guardsmen had violated. Mitchell even had the gall to say he was satisfied "that the Department has taken every possible action to serve justice." For most Americans that was, at long last, the end of the Kent State problem.

Early in 1972, James F. Ahern, another member of the Scranton Commission and formerly a police chief of New Haven, Connecticut, said that the only question that had to be answered about Kent State and Jackson State was whether or not the crime committed by those who shot and killed unarmed students was murder or manslaughter. Only someone with a deep cynicism concerning our system of justice, he went on to say, could assume that persons killed unnecessarily and inexcusably had not been killed illegally.

The Nixon Administration, by its inaction, has demonstrated its deep cynicism concerning our system of justice. Surely there was some reason for the shootings at Kent State, but John Mitchell and his successor, Richard Kleindienst, have stubbornly refused to permit the machinery of law and order to ascertain conclusively what that reason was. Officially, the Justice Department has ruled out self-defense, and General Canterbury admitted to the Scranton Commission that his men did not panic. We are left, then, with the strong possibility of a willful act on the part of a few guardsmen. We are left with these words of James Michener: "We know almost exactly what happened, save the crucial matter of whether there was, at the practice field, any kind of order or agreement which triggered the firing a few moments later."

How much longer are the American people willing to let the questions surrounding these brutal deaths go unresolved? Indefinitely? Perhaps so, but we hope this book will sufficiently prod your conscience to demand that your government use the investigative and judicial tools at its disposal to find out, at least, *why* four young people lost their lives at Kent State.

one
Prelude
to Violence

As the Ohio law says,
use any force that's
necessary even to the
point of shooting. We
don't want to get into
that but the law says
that we can if neces-
sary.

Major General
Sylvester Del Corso
Press conference,
May 3, 1970

On April 30, 1970, President Nixon announced over national television that a massive American–South Vietnamese troop offensive into Cambodia was in progress. The objective was the North Vietnamese sanctuaries and their headquarters for military operations in South Vietnam. "We take this action," the President said, "not for the purpose of expanding the war into Cambodia but for the purpose of ending the war in Vietnam." These were familiar words to a war-weary public. To many students this meant a return to President Johnson's earlier hopes for a military victory. When Nixon said he "would rather be a one-term President" and do what he considered right than be a "two-term President at the cost of seeing America become a second-rate power and seeing this nation accept the first defeat in its proud 190-year history," the groans on numerous campuses that night turned into impassioned and sometimes violent protests the next day.

At Kent State University in Ohio, however, the anti-war demonstration on May 1 was quiet, dignified, and peaceful. A group of history students gathered at noon around the Victory Bell on the Commons, the traditional site for rallies. The organizers of this protest symbolically buried a copy of the Constitution which someone had hastily torn from a book for the ceremony. This rally was typical of demonstrations on this essentially non-political Midwestern campus, inspiring no more than about five hundred out of some twenty thousand enrolled students to attend.

Three hours later, the Black United Students held a rally which had been called before President Nixon's announcement. Some four hundred showed up to hear black students from Ohio State University talk about the recent disorders on their campus and their experiences with the Ohio National Guard. The meeting broke up in about forty-five minutes. Kent State that day was as quiet as its history indicated it would be, and late that afternoon President Robert White departed for Iowa to visit his sister-in-law and attend a Sunday meeting of the American College Testing Program.

Kent State has been called a "suitcase university" because many students leave the campus for weekends at home. Friday was the day of this exodus. May 1, 1970, was no exception. During that afternoon and evening there was "a steady stream of traffic leaving and entering the city of Kent." As is the case in most college towns in America, Kent has a considerable number of bars, many of them located on North Water Street, "the Strip," as it is called. It is to this part of Kent that scores of those students who are staying on campus through the weekend go on Friday evenings. This particular night was no exception there either. Only the weather was different—the first really warm evening of the year.

Nothing untoward happened until about eleven that evening, "when a motorcycle gang, 'The Chosen Few,' began to perform tricks on their bikes for the people lining North Water Street." With the temperature in the seventies, the mood of the students was festive rather than restive and not many were rapping about the invasion of Cambodia. As Joe Eszterhas and Michael D. Roberts describe the scene in *Thirteen Seconds:* "Many inside the bars watched the New York Knickerbockers and the Los Angeles Lakers battle in the NBA playoffs. A group pitched pennies outside a bar. A few began dancing in a circle on the sidewalk and overspilled into the street." With fewer than ten men on duty that night, Kent Police Chief Roy Thompson had only two patrol cars out and every so often one of the cars would cruise by along "the Strip." At 11:27 the first in a series of escalating incidents occurred when someone threw a beer can at one of the passing police cars.

After the shooting, much was made of the bonfire started in the street that Friday night, because of the burning that was to follow the next day, when the ROTC building on campus was destroyed. Most people assumed that students were responsible for the bonfire. They were not. "Some of the 'Chosen Few' collected trash in the middle of Water Street and built a bonfire. Gang members took turns urinating into the fire and doing stunts around it with their cycles."

Violence flared when a middle-aged man drove a new Oldsmobile through obstacles and people. The revelers had closed the street illegally for their so-called festival. When the man drove through the crowd, the mood of the festivities changed.

Chanting against the war and Nixon, some twenty students started throwing bottles at store windows. This vandalism continued until all windows along North Water Street, except one, were shattered. The senseless destruction did not compare with the kind of mayhem that follows big Midwest college football games, but the vandalism coupled with the refrain "One, two, three, four, we don't want your fucking war" was enough to convince Kent Mayor LeRoy Satrom and Thompson that their town was on the verge of serious disorder. At 12:30 in the morning Satrom declared a state of civil emergency and arbitrarily ordered all bars closed. Chief Thompson summoned his entire force of twenty-one men to duty and alerted the Portage County sheriff's office. With commendable alacrity, Thompson assembled fifteen policemen and fifteen sheriff's deputies, equipped to handle riots. The force advanced into North Water Street, where a crowd of some four hundred to five hundred retreated before them. Thompson executed the mayor's order by forcibly ejecting from all bars hundreds who had not participated in the street revels. This action inevitably angered those who had been separated from their drinks and those who had already paid a cover charge for entertainment. The action also swelled the size of the crowd with these understandably incensed individuals.

At 12:47 A.M., Satrom phoned the office of Governor James A. Rhodes in Columbus and told John McElroy, the governor's administrative assistant, that "SDS students had taken over a portion of Kent." This erroneous and alarming information prompted McElroy to call Major General Sylvester Del Corso, adjutant general of the Ohio National Guard. Del Corso called his liaison officer, Lieutenant Charles J. Barnette, and the machinery that was to lead to shooting and death was set in motion that first hour of Saturday, May 2. Subsequent official investigations were unable to find any convincing evidence to support Satrom's grounds for appealing to the governor for help in combatting the "SDS threat." Had Satrom and Thompson acted more on facts and less on rumors, a few dozen bottle-throwing students could have been subdued and arrested *without* military assistance.

Between one and two o'clock the thirty law-enforcement officers, with the help of tear gas, cleared the downtown area, and an hour later all was quiet. However, Satrom had called the governor, and Lieutenant Barnette of the Ohio National Guard would be arriving in Kent in a few hours to assess the situation.

On campus, a window in the ROTC building had been broken and the culprit, Michael Weekly, apprehended. (For this offense Weekly was later tried, convicted, and sentenced to thirty days' imprisonment.) By three o'clock the campus, too, was quiet. None of the four students who were about to die had participated in the events of this night. The next morning, in fact, a considerable number of students went downtown to help storekeepers clear up the mess and repair the damage.

As this was happening, Mayor Satrom was formalizing the state of civil emergency he had declared and imposing a curfew from 8 P.M. to 6 A.M. Later he amended the curfew for the campus to 1 A.M. to 6 A.M. and provided for students to lawfully assemble and peacefully demonstrate on campus. Not surprisingly, poor communications, rumor, and inaccurate leaflets led some students to think that the curfew for the town did not start until 1 A.M. and other students to believe that they were going to be confined to their rooms on Saturday night from 8 P.M. to 6 A.M. This confusion was further compounded when the university administration, in White's absence, obtained an injunction, naming Michael Weekly and some five hundred John Does, which prohibited further damage to campus property. Robert E. Matson, Vice President for Student Affairs, explained it to the student body in still another leaflet distributed on campus. Some twelve thousand copies of the leaflet were issued, but the thousands of students who were away for the weekend never saw it until their return Sunday night and Monday morning, just a few hours before the fatal gunfire.

In Kent, Mayor Satrom announced that the destruction of Friday night had cost storekeepers $50,000; after the shooting, this figure was revised to $15,000. In the midst of all this, the Ohio National Guard's liaison officer arrived and met with Matson at eleven. The university official "was visibly surprised" to learn that Lieutenant Barnette's unit, the 145th Infantry Regiment, had been put on alert for possible duty in Kent.

Matson explained to Barnette that the university had its own procedure to be put into effect in the event of a riot situation. "First, the university police would be called in. Second, the Portage County Sheriff's Department would be called in. And then, only if absolutely necessary, the Ohio State Highway Patrol would be called in." But, the lieutenant told Matson, such a plan could not be implemented if the National Guard was called in, because the Guard would take over "complete control" of both the town and the campus. Barnette's stand ran counter to the Army's field manual for civil-disturbance duty, which categorically states, as does the Ohio constitution, that the role of the militia in civil disorders shall be solely supportive of civilian law-enforcement forces and can assume the kind of control Barnette was talking about only if and when martial law is declared by the governor of the state. The lieutenant's ill-advised and ill-informed remark prompted Matson to call President White in Iowa.

Evidently White was disturbed by Matson's report and ordered him to send the university's twin-engine plane for him. Ironically, the Kent State police force, numbering thirty-three men, was "the largest and best-equipped full-time security force in Portage County," and the Ohio State Highway Patrol, which the university, as a state educational institution, could call upon but Satrom could not, was the most professional law-enforcement agency in the state of Ohio, particularly in coping with civil disorders. Obviously, these jurisdictional problems could have been satisfactorily resolved but for Barnette's statement that the National Guard, once called, would have authority over the town and the university. Satrom wanted the Guard, and, once committed, they should have remained in the town, under Satrom's control, for the purpose of enforcing his curfew. As for the campus, the university's own police and, if absolutely necessary, the Ohio Highway Patrol, should have had sole jurisdiction.

Barnette later met with Mayor Satrom and gave him until five o'clock to decide whether he needed military assistance. Although both town and campus had been quiet throughout the day, rumors were being fed into the mayor's office at an alarming pace. "Weathermen had been observed on campus and positively identified. There was evidence of guns on campus. There were plans to burn down the city of Kent. Special targets would be the banks, the post office, the campus ROTC building. LSD would be placed in the water supply."

Instead of passing this "intelligence" on to university officials so that they might take whatever action was deemed necessary, Satrom turned directly to Columbus and asked for troops. One Kent State official later described these events: "We were a driverless car racing downhill without brakes." They were indeed, and neither the town nor the university adequately communicated with each other to work out a plan for diverting the car.

Vice President Matson was unaware of Satrom's appeal for the National Guard. Not having heard from the mayor, or from Lieutenant Barnette, Matson assumed that the crisis—if there ever had been a crisis—had passed. He sent an aide to inquire of campus police chief Donald Schwartzmiller and other university security officials whether "they had sufficient manpower to keep order on the campus. 'No sweat' was the reply." Matson arranged for several on-campus activities that night, including a dance to be held at the Tri-Towers complex, and he was confident that the rally that was to take place on the Commons at 8 P.M. would not draw more than the usual two or three percent of the students. Although the rally would not be in violation of the mayor's state of civil emergency, Matson issued a circular listing the activities arranged for the students who could not go into Kent after eight o'clock and recommending that they consider the wisdom of not attending the rally. Only when Chester Williams, Kent State's Director of Safety and Public Services, and Richard Dunn, Vice President for Financial Affairs, returned to the campus did Matson learn that Satrom had called for the National Guard. Williams and Dunn assured Matson, however, that the troops had been requested "for duty only in Kent, not on the Kent State campus."

By 7:30 Saturday night, a crowd of about six hundred had gathered on the Commons. "The group appeared to be an idle collection of students whom the curfew had prevented from going downtown." Schwartzmiller decided to call the Ohio State Highway Patrol as a precautionary measure. He was advised that the patrol could not enter the campus "unless arrests were necessary." Schwartzmiller replied that "there was no basis for arrests at that time." In stark contrast to the alarming information being fed into the mayor's office, Matson was receiving intelligence which finally convinced him that it was no longer necessary for Kent State President White to come back from Iowa. He called White and told him that "it looked as if it would be a routine night." In reality, however, Matson's information, too, was misleading. The crowd on the Commons had aroused itself into conducting a tour of the campus to round up more supporters, and by the time they came back, they were "around one thousand" strong.

The question whether the crowd was organized and led by revolutionaries has since become the subject of heated debate. Some insist that a "substantial cadre of hard-core radical leaders and perhaps one or two revolutionaries" had "their eyes on much more than the rickety old ROTC building." Utter nonsense, say Eszterhas and Roberts, who were reporters for the Cleveland *Plain Dealer* at the time, and neither the Justice Department nor the President's Commission on Campus Unrest found evidence to support the claim. Obviously there were some agitators in the crowd, but that is quite different from "hard-core" radicals and "revolutionaries" bent on "much more" than committing arson on the ROTC building. Official reports confirm that the agitators were few in number but very vocal. As the crowd neared ROTC, one of them shouted, "Get it," and the cry was picked up by a few more, who hollered, "Burn it," and "ROTC has to go."

The next hour is shrouded in confusion. Few reports agree on exactly what happened, primarily because of conflicting testimony on the part of witnesses. Michener attached considerable significance to the burning of an American flag that night. The President's commission says "someone burned a miniature American flag." The Justice Department says "an American flag was burned." Eszterhas and Roberts reported that a demonstrator "unfurled an American flag, ripped it, and set it afire. Holding the burning flag aloft, he walked toward the cheering mob. 'Right on!' the crowd yelled." And Michener—he says, "At 8:26 P.M. a young man who may have been a student, but whom none of the marshals were able to identify, whipped a fair-sized American flag from around his middle, where he had been carrying it, fastened it to a makeshift pole which he had secreted down an arm of his coat, and set it ablaze with a cigarette lighter. It burned slowly. Then, as the crowd cheered, it burst into vigorous flame and made a compelling picture against the evening sky." The sharp contrast among the descriptions of that flag reflects the conflict that surrounds almost every incident of these four days. Even the criminal burning down of the ROTC building remains a subject for dispute because it is unclear whether the building was destroyed by student arsonists or other provocateurs, and how much of the damage resulted from police neglect.

While the crowd stood around watching, a couple of dozen persons, of which "a significant proportion were not Kent State students," attempted to set fire to the old barracks building. When the crowd drifted away from the scene and some two hundred headed toward the town to challenge the curfew, the few fires started in different parts of the building had died out, but when they returned to the Commons the structure was a blazing inferno.

All reports agree that the Kent Fire Department was notified at 8:49. That was quick action on someone's part: the ROTC building "did not begin to burn until 8:45 P.M." Or was it earlier? The Justice Department reports that at "8:30 P.M. the building was on fire." No, it wasn't, according to the President's commission; it was "8:45 P.M." James Michener says "the fire at ROTC was well ablaze" at 8:49, but the Justice Department says that when Schwartzmiller's police arrived on the scene, "the firemen left the ROTC, which was not yet ablaze." The time was approximately 9 P.M., according to the Justice Department. Schwartzmiller insists that when his men arrived, the building was not even afire.

Michener concedes that at 9:27 "the building was merely smoldering," but at 9:45, he says, "a preposterous thing happened." The smoldering building "burst into flame at many points." How this happened is unclear, but it could not have happened at a more inopportune moment: the advance units of the Ohio National Guard were entering Kent.

Vice President Matson assumed that the Ohio Highway Patrol, summoned to the campus since the burning constituted an arrestable offense, would restore order. He was amazed to hear over a police radio that "the Guard is moving into Kent." With President White in Iowa, it was up to Matson to ensure that the Highway Patrol maintained jurisdiction over the campus and the Guard stayed in the town, but the fire against the sky drew the generals like moths to a flame, and within an hour the National Guard occupied the campus as well as the town.

General Del Corso, learning that the firemen's first efforts had been interrupted by students pulling on hoses and throwing stones at the men, ordered the students back to the campus with what is reported by Eszterhas and Roberts as "a terse command to his troops: 'Shoot any rioter who cuts a fire hose.'" Shoot him! Not arrest him. And so the guardsmen went onto the campus, though neither Del Corso nor his deputy, General Canterbury, had requested permission of any university official.

Before the Guard entered the campus, there was a clash between some demonstrators who had been dispersed from the Commons by campus police and some members of Troop G of the 107th Armored Cavalry on their way to the university. The windshield of a jeep was shattered by a rock and SP/4 Ronald West was "cut in the mouth by glass."* Seven more guardsmen were injured (or so they later claimed) by flying glass, and eventually tear gas was used to drive the demonstrators, estimated at about two hundred, back to the campus. How many of these were not students is not known. The Justice Department reports that many of those who were at the scene of the ROTC fire left for the town when the barracks did not burn, and, as already noted, a significant proportion of these were not Kent State students.

The Ohio National Guard arrived on the Commons shortly after ten o'clock that evening. The crowd on campus, now down to some five hundred, had retreated from the vicinity of the ruined ROTC building up to the crest of the hill by Taylor Hall. Half an hour later, the generals formed their men into a skirmish line and sent them out with fixed bayonets and tear gas to disperse the students. Some rocks were thrown, and guardsmen chased a number of demonstrators. "A 21-year-old senior suffered an eight-inch bayonet cut on his right cheek and a deep stab wound in the leg when two guardsmen chased him up against the Johnson Hall wall."

Official reports confirm that Del Corso's sweep of the campus accomplished its objective sometime between 11:00 and 11:55 that evening, when the general phoned his staff headquarters at Fort Hayes and advised that the "situation at Kent is under control." What these reports do not tell us is that Del Corso participated in the rock throwing. As reported by Ezsterhas and Roberts, as Del Corso and his men neared the area around the Tri-Towers building, southeast of Taylor Hall, a rock landed near his feet. The general, "sweating and angry, bent down, picked up the rock, and threw it high over the heads of troops in front of him. Cleveland *Plain Dealer* reporter Carl Kovac heard him say, 'Throw 'em back at those bastards,' as he threw the rock. Kent State student Martin Kurta, a former member of the student government, heard him say, 'If those goddamn kids can throw rocks, I can, too.' " So much for professionalism in the Ohio National Guard.

The burning of the ROTC building was the most serious act of violence during the four days until the guardsmen shot and killed four students. We still do not know who was responsible, and Ohio's much publicized indictment of students and others for arson, interfering with firemen, and other offenses related to the crime suddenly collapsed in November 1971 when the state's attorney general dropped all charges against twenty of the twenty-five initially indicted. The Justice Department reports that the FBI "identified 13 persons involved in the burning of the ROTC building and the harassment of

---

* This guardsman's injuries are noted in the Ohio National Guard's roster of injuries sustained on May 4, 1970.

firemen; some of the identified persons are high school students from Ohio who were possibly on LSD at the time of the burning. One person is alleged to be the principal narcotics peddler in Kent. None of the victims of the shooting incident have been implicated in the unlawful burning of the ROTC building."

During the early hours of Sunday morning the scene on the campus was one of military occupation. Most guardsmen no more wanted to be there than the students wanted them there. Questionable judgment had sent into Kent several units of guardsmen who had been on tense active duty in Cleveland since Wednesday trying to restore order between rival factions in a bitter truckers' strike. Many of the guardsmen had already coped with attacks by rock- and bottle-throwing strikers and, on one occasion, had actually been shot at. In addition, their ranks had suffered numerous injuries. It is not difficult to imagine the mood prevailing among some of the guardsmen when they were pulled out of the Cleveland strike crisis and ordered into Kent, where they were welcomed with more rocks and sustained new injuries. This time, however, it wasn't striking truckmen but demonstrating students. To a few guardsmen there was a distinct difference.

The decision of Governor Rhodes to use these tired units was bitterly criticized by Stephen M. Young, then the senior senator from Ohio. Young accused Rhodes of committing an "abominable blunder" in summoning these guardsmen to Kent when there were "two companies of Ohio National Guard Military Police, located only twenty miles from Kent at Warren, that were trained in riot control." The wildcat strike was settled at six o'clock Saturday night, and as Young points out, the guardsmen expected to return to their homes for the rest of the weekend, not to be sent into another civil disturbance, when most of them had had only a few hours' sleep during the preceding forty-eight hours. The decision made by Rhodes was indeed a grave error of judgment, evincing little concern for the welfare of either guardsmen or students.

With sunrise came the full awareness of the extent to which the Ohio National Guard had taken over. Although Sunday, May 3, was quiet, until the late evening, the presence of armored personnel carriers, army trucks and jeeps, and combat-equipped troops did little to ease the undercurrent of tension. Mark Harris, a student who would later work with others in behalf of the Kent State Medical Fund, dryly observed that when he went to get a drink from the water cooler they even had a soldier with an M-1 rifle guarding it.

Local officials had been preparing themselves most of Sunday morning for the arrival of Governor Rhodes, and amid all the pompous rhetoric that was spouted, only one official said anything intelligent. "I'm going to try and close that school down," Portage County Prosecutor Ronald J. Kane told a sheriff's deputy. "I'm afraid we're in for trouble if we don't." Kane had not reckoned with the governor's determination to capitalize on the situation. Rhodes needed votes, especially that weekend after polls had shown him trailing Robert Taft, Jr., in their race for the Republican nomination to run for retiring Stephen Young's seat in the U.S. Senate. Primary day was May 5, and there were strong indications that the voters in populous Cuyahoga County had responded favorably to the governor's show of force at Ohio State University and now Kent State.

President White also arrived in Kent this day, and he would accept without question the governor's decision to keep the university open. White was well aware "that Rhodes was two days away from a primary test that could end his political career, desperately riding a last-minute law and order campaign train, and that Kent provided the governor with a perfect statewide stage for his table-thumping theatrics." And table-thump he did at the news conference that took place at Firehouse No. 1 in the town of Kent.

In addition to Rhodes, there were General Del Corso, Mayor Satrom, Prosecutor Kane, Kent Police Chief Thompson, and other state and local officials. Michener reports that a witness to the governor's news conference said that the moment the press insisted on a conference "Jim Rhodes changed completely. He became a candidate for the United States Senate. He has always been very much a take-charge guy, and I think he wanted to show the voters of Ohio that he was not going to be pushed around by a lot of young punks." As Michener himself noted, this was the governor's "last chance to make points" in the forthcoming primary.

The significance of the Rhodes speech cannot be ignored, especially in light of the atmosphere in which it was delivered and the fact that it was not only broadcast to the voters but also beamed into the National Guard's bivouac area on campus, where tempers were as high among some of the soldiers as they were down at the firehouse. It was an incredibly irresponsible harangue, as these extracts confirm:

> The scene here that the city of Kent is facing is probably the most vicious form of campus-oriented violence yet perpetrated by dissident groups and their allies in the state of Ohio . . . Now it ceases to be a problem of the colleges in Ohio. This now is the problem of the state of Ohio. Now we're going to put a stop to this, for this reason. The same group that we're dealing with here today, and there's three or four of them, they only have one thing in mind. That is to destroy higher education in Ohio . . . Last night I think that we have seen all forms of violence, the worst. And when they start taking over communities, this is when we're going to use every weapon of the law-enforcement agencies of Ohio to drive them out of Kent. We have these same groups going from one campus to the other, and they use the universities that are supported by the taxpayers of Ohio as a sanctuary. And in this they make definite plans of burning, destroying, and throwing rocks at police and at the National Guard and the Highway Patrol . . . They're

21

worse than the brownshirts and the Communist element and also the night riders and the vigilantes. They're the worst type of people that we harbor in America . . . It's over with in Ohio . . . I think that we're up against the strongest, well-trained, militant revolutionary group that has ever assembled in America . . . We are going to eradicate the problem, we're not going to treat the symptoms.

If it was unclear just what the governor meant by "every weapon" and "eradicate the problem," General Del Corso clarified it for the newsmen. "As the Ohio law says," the general pointed out, "use any force that's necessary even to the point of shooting. We don't want to get into that, but the law says that we can if necessary." Coming from a major general who had shown his men how to throw rocks at students, this statement marked the high point of officialdom's contribution to restoring order and calming tension. The next remark by the governor set the tone for the following twenty-four hours: "No one is safe in Portage County. It is just that simple. No one is safe and I, I do not believe that people understand the seriousness of these individuals who are organized in a revolutionary frame of mind."

In essence, what Governor Rhodes had said to the guardsmen was: You men are up against the scum of America but be careful. They are vicious, organized, and dangerous. Your job is to protect the citizens of Kent and Portage County, where no one will be safe if we fail, and remember, your commanding officer has said, we can stop them with gunfire if necessary.

In retrospect, it is hardly surprising that the guns did fire, that thirteen of "the worst type of people we harbor in America" were shot, four of them fatally.

James Michener turned to the dean of the Kent State Honors College, Myron J. Lunine, for an appraisal of campus reaction to the Rhodes speech. Lunine, a professor of political science and "one of the coolest heads on the faculty," cautioned Michener not to forget that the students had suffered "four heavy psychological blows in a row. Their President had termed them 'bums.' He had sent troops into Cambodia when the announced plan of our government was the withdrawal of troops from Vietnam. Armed troops were occupying the campus. And now the governor of the state was calling them worse than Brown Shirts. Do you honestly wonder that many of them felt a deep sense of revulsion?" Michener recognized that these blows had "caused despair among many of the most stable students at the university." He quotes one girl as saying, "If the President thinks I'm a bum and the governor thinks I'm a Nazi, what does it matter how I act?" However, he does not criticize the governor's ill-advised remarks. To Michener, Rhodes's speech was in "the flamboyant tradition of American political leadership and cannot be faulted for that." The speech may well have been traditional flamboyant politics, but it was very much out of place at Kent that Sunday with eight hundred combat-equipped troops in the area with empty stomachs and minds dulled by lack of sleep. Words were very important that weekend, Dr. Lunine told Michener.

Sunday afternoon at Kent State was a scene of tranquillity and friendliness. Jeff Sallot, a journalist who witnessed the shooting and who is now a reporter for the Toronto *Star,* described that afternoon to Michener: "What a lovely day it was, real springtime. All the coeds were out for the first time in their spring dresses and no coats, and they made a great hit with the guardsmen. There was a lot of flirting and a little surreptitious hand-holding. No fear, no anxiety, no animosity. The bad language of the preceding night was forgotten and all we heard were idle rumors of the most gentle kind. 'Guard's going to leave campus this evening.' I certainly expected them to be gone by morning."

Among those coeds strolling around the campus was Allison Krause. Accompanied by a young man she had met six months earlier, Barry Levine, she spotted a young guardsman with a flower in the end of the barrel of his M-1 rifle. Barry and she went over to the soldier and struck up a conversation with him. The three were talking when an officer appeared and ordered the guardsman to remove the flower. He obeyed, but to Allison this was just one more instance, among so many, of the attitude of the military that the campus was foreign territory and the students some kind of enemy. When the officer dressed down Guardsman Myers, it was too much for the spirited young woman. "Flowers are better than bullets," she shouted after the departing officer—who simply ignored her.

For all the surface appearance of calm, forces were at work that set the stage for a sit-in demonstration that night and violence the next day. Before Governor Rhodes departed from Kent, he announced his intention of seeking a state-of-emergency injunction to apply to both town and campus. When Prosecutor Kane attempted to close the university for a cooling-off period, Rhodes rebuffed him; Kane would be playing into the hands of the SDS and the Weathermen who sought to close down Kent State. No one had produced any evidence to support this assumption, but this failed to move either Kane or President White to challenge the governor.

As it happened, Rhodes never did seek or obtain the injunction, so the only state-of-emergency decree that existed up to the time of the noon rally on May 4 was Mayor Satrom's, and his proclamation specifically permitted "peaceful assembly, demonstration, dissent or movement about the campus." Both the Justice Department and the Scranton Commission concluded that the noon rally was indeed a peaceful assembly. Nevertheless, the general impression in the minds of the public is that the students were lawfully prohibited from holding the rally and that in holding it they had violated the law and must therefore accept the consequences. This impression is due in no small part to erroneous reporting by a number of television commentators and newspaper reporters that the May 4 rally "violated martial law." Even the discredited, and eventually destroyed, report of the Ohio grand jury went out of its way to state that "the Ohio National Guard was called solely for the purpose of assisting the civil authority. At no time during the period of May 1st through May 4th was martial law declared." The first part of this conclusion was contrary to the facts, because the Guard was assisting no one. But it satisfied the requirements of Ohio law, which specifically prohibits the militia from assuming complete control in civil disturbances unless martial law has been declared. The second part simply confirms the fact that Rhodes never did obtain his state-of-emergency injunction.

After the Rhodes press conference, Vice President Matson's executive assistant, John Huffman, an attorney, had asked Major Harry Jones of the Ohio National Guard what the governor's injunction meant. Jones, who was not the Guard's legal officer, said he would find out. He disappeared for a few minutes, and then, from what Jones said, Huffman "received the impression that the state of emergency permitted 'no gatherings or rallies at all.' This was a fatal misinterpretation. The only proclamation in effect was Mayor Satrom's State of Civil Emergency which did not prohibit assembly." Instead of verifying the major's opinion with the National Guard legal officer, Huffman told Matson what Jones had said, and Matson, together with student-body president Frank Frisina, issued a "special message" to the students. This leaflet categorically stated that the violence of the previous two days had led to "the Governor's imposition of a state of emergency encompassing both the city of Kent *and* the University." Rhodes had done no such thing, nor did he do so later. The rest of the Matson-Frisina statement was equally erroneous:

> The Governor, through the National Guard, has assumed legal control of the campus and the city of Kent. As currently defined the state of emergency has established the following:
> 1. Prohibited all forms of outdoor demonstrations and rallies peaceful or otherwise.
> 2. Empowered the National Guard to make arrests.
> 3. A curfew is in effect for the city from 8:00 P.M. to 6:00 A.M. and an on-campus curfew from 1:00 A.M. has been ordered by the National Guard. [This, too, was nonsense. These were the curfews contained in Mayor Satrom's state of civil emergency issued before the National Guard arrived in Kent.]
> The above will remain in effect until altered or removed by order of the Governor.

The only accurate information in this document are the curfew hours.

Rhodes had told the press that he was going to "ask for an injunction" which he described as "equivalent to a state of emergency." The

Scranton Commission later found "no official record that such an injunction was ever sought or obtained." The Justice Department could only report that it was "not known what person(s) decided that assemblies of all kinds would be prohibited nor do we know under what authority this decision was made, nor what distribution the [Matson-Frisina] 'special message' received." What we do know is that twelve thousand copies of the "special message" were run off. And indeed, Governor Rhodes's order committing the Ohio National Guard to the town of Kent, and the campus, did not become official until May 5, the day after the thirteen students were shot. The proclamation "providing written authorization for the commitment of National Guard troops to the city of Kent" was signed by the governor's chief administrative assistant, John McElroy, after the fact.

The Scranton Commission investigators learned that some students completely ignored the "special message" because it was signed by Matson and Frisina. "Many students," the commission reported, "remained confused all day Sunday about the rules governing the campus and what they permitted." The first challenge to the Matson-Frisina interpretation of Major Jones's opinion on Governor Rhodes's intention to do what he did not do came that Sunday evening at Prentice Gate when several hundred students staged a sit-in protest. The demonstrators demanded that President White and Mayor Satrom meet with them. Once again official intransigence held sway. Both men refused to meet with the students. In the case of the mayor, this was to be expected. His first consideration was the citizens of Kent, not the students. But for White to refuse is another thing altogether.

President White had done little, if anything, visibly to assert his authority as president of Kent State University and fulfill his obligations to the parents whose sons and daughters were on his campus. Instead of utilizing the power of his office to ensure that the National Guard on campus acted strictly in support of campus police and, once they were summoned, of the Ohio Highway Patrol, White went on campus radio and said: "Events have taken decisions out of our hands." This remark typifies the role he played in the brief time he was at Kent State during the four days. And on Monday he showed by deed the extent of his concern for the safety and well-being of the students in his charge. Knowing that General Canterbury was sending armed troops to disperse the noon rally, White, accompanied by his vice presidents, Matson and Roskens, left the campus and went to the Brown Derby restaurant in Kent. There, Joe Eszterhas says, the sound of gunfire interrupted their lunch.

The Prentice Gate sit-in began on the Commons at about eight that evening. The gathering crowd was peaceful, according to Scranton Commission findings, and "included a group of coeds kicking a soccer ball around." As would be the case the following day, however, as the size of the crowd increased, so did the alarm of the authorities, regardless of how the students were conducting themselves. Both the campus police and the Ohio Highway Patrol suggested to Colonel Harold Finley, the National Guard officer in charge during the absence of Del Corso and Canterbury, that Mayor Satrom's I A.M. campus curfew "be cancelled and an immediate curfew imposed." Apparently none of these men in authority gave serious thought to the problems involved in informing a population of some twenty thousand people of these sudden changes of curfew times, regulations, and proclamations.

No one consulted the mayor about the proposal to amend the curfew hours for the campus, and shortly before nine o'clock the National Guard's self-elected authority on legal matters, Major Jones, read the Ohio Riot Act to the crowd on the Commons and gave them five minutes to disperse. Again let me stress that the crowd was peaceful and presumably aware that Mayor Satrom's proclamation permitted "peaceful assembly, demonstration, dissent or movement about the campus." They ignored Jones, so the National Guard attacked them with tear gas and fixed bayonets. As the crowd scattered, one group headed for the home of President White and another for Prentice Gate.

At White's residence, the students were driven off by tear gas, but at the Gate a sizable crowd assembled opposite a line of National Guardsmen. The request to see White was transmitted to Vice President Matson and his associate, Ronald Roskens, Vice President for Administration. The two men "rejected the idea"; "they felt that the Guard was in charge of the campus and there was no point in negotiating in the streets."

At eleven the Ohio Riot Act was again read to the crowd, this time by Colonel Finley. "The students, previously nonviolent, became hostile," the Scranton Commission reports. "They felt that they had been double-crossed. They cursed the guardsmen and police and threw rocks at them. Tear gas was fired and the crowd ran back from the gate across the campus lawn."

As students fled from Prentice Gate, guardsmen pursued them with fixed bayonets. Neither the Justice Department nor the Scranton Commission paid much attention to the injuries inflicted on both men and women students by guardsmen with their bayonets, nor did they note the anger these brutal acts aroused among those who witnessed them. Michener reports that "at least two and probably seven students" were bayoneted and that "a white boy and a black girl were taken to the hospital, and these were put on record, but there were other incidents." One girl, who was bayoneted outside the library, testified before the Kent State Commission. She had been at home most of the weekend and, after returning to campus late Sunday evening, had walked out to the front campus with a friend to have a look at the sit-down. She described the scene:

26

Many people started running for the library. Somehow the windows were opened and kids were stuffing themselves through them. There was confusion. It was frightening. We started walking toward the library. I did not panic, for in all my naive upbringing, I had a total trust that the National Guard would never touch us, for we had done nothing wrong. We stood against the library wall along with others to wait until they passed. About ten of the Guardsmen were grouped together near the building as they approached. We were among the first students to be encountered by them. I was still confident that they would not touch us. Then I saw their faces. There was hate; and it was coming towards me in the form of swinging rifle butts and bayonets. They were yelling, "Get back, get back!" Get back to where, I do not know, for the hard-core demonstrators were at the other end of the front campus. There was no where to go—we were encircled by Guardsmen. *There was no provocation.* Before I knew it, they were on us. Sometime between hearing them shout and being pushed through a library window by a fellow student, squashing someone else in the process, I was bayoneted in the lower abdomen and in the right leg. The leg was only deeply scratched and bruised; the abdomen was punctured. This all happened in a matter of seconds. I didn't actually realize I was hurt till I was in the library, when I saw something was very wrong. I still didn't know how badly, though. There were others there who had been hit badly by rifle butts . . .

The stretcher-bearers who removed the injured girl from the library attracted attention, and word of the bayoneting spread rapidly on campus, increasing the already festering antagonism of students toward the Guard.

While guardsmen chased students across the campus to the accompaniment of exploding M-79 grenade launchers firing tear gas, a helicopter hovered overhead, the shattering whop-whop-whop of its blades adding the final ingredient to a scene right out of Vietnam. The helicopter's searchlight played back and forth over the campus as its wash spread the tear gas into dormitory rooms and corridors. Of the four students who had only hours to live, only Jeffrey Miller witnessed the sit-in at Prentice Gate. Like the girl who was bayoneted, Jeff left when the Guard moved out and started firing tear gas. Sandy Scheuer "decided to stay home and study," as did Bill Schroeder. The Scranton Commission erroneously implied, as did the Justice Department report, that Allison Krause had participated in the sit-in. She had not; she was in Johnson Hall at that time, engaged in a private altercation with some student counselors over two empty soda bottles. James Michener describes the scene in considerable detail in his book. When she and Barry Levine left Johnson Hall, the National Guard had already begun to disperse the crowd at Prentice Gate. She and Barry were walking toward Tri-Towers across the football field, along with about fifteen other people, when a contingent of a dozen or so guardsmen came running across the crest of the hill between Taylor and Prentice halls. "They were yelling," Barry said, and they had fixed bayonets. "Everyone ran for the fence," he continued, "which skirts the eastern side of the field, and tried to get through the small opening, but I realized we were all not going to make it before the guardsmen would be upon us." He grabbed Allison's arm and together they ran the length of the fence until they got around it and headed for Tri-Towers. It was at this time that much of the crowd fleeing Prentice Gate appeared on the scene, which led to the inaccurate statement in the commission's report that among the "fleeing Kent State students" from Prentice Gate "was Allison Krause."

By one o'clock Monday morning the campus was once again quiet. Fifty-one persons had been arrested for curfew violations. The helicopter still buzzed overhead, and tear gas pervaded many of the campus buildings. Students who had been away for the weekend started to arrive back, many of them completely ignorant of what had happened. Mostly by other students, they were informed of the tear gasing and the bayoneting, acts which made the burning of the ROTC building seem insignificant to some of them. Just as officials had demonstrated contempt for the rights of the students, so some students demonstrated contempt for the officials' genuine concern about arson, a serious crime. The root problem at Kent State was lack of communication, and as the days passed, this problem grew more and more grave, as Phillip K. Tompkins and Elaine Vandem Bout Anderson show in their impressive study, *Communications Crisis at Kent State.* When finally the students demanded a meeting, they were answered with tear gas, and in turn the guardsmen were answered with rocks. With everyone shouting at one another, no one could be heard, until the forces unleashed by official ineptitude, inflammatory political rhetoric, and arson crystallized into a burst of gunfire.

Three nights of violence had made it appear to the students that the National Guard was acting independently of all civilian authority. Whenever students began to assemble in sizable numbers, the Ohio Riot Act was read to them by the Guard, in direct violation of Mayor Satrom's state of civil emergency. The burning of the ROTC building called for prompt police action and immediate arrest of those responsible. Instead, the police surrendered their authority to the National Guard, who simply moved against all students, innocent and guilty alike, without lawful powers to do so. Tear gas and bayonets against everyone and anyone were substituted for professional law enforcement. Such conduct set the stage for the biggest peaceful assembly in the history of Kent State University, a demonstration to protest, not the war, not Cambodia, but the continued presence of the Ohio National Guard on the campus.

two
What Happened on May 4

These students are going to have to find out what law and order is all about.

Brigadier General
Robert Canterbury
Noon, May 4, 1970

Between midnight and 1 A.M. on Monday, May 4, Troop G of the 2nd Squadron, 107th Armored Cavalry of the Ohio National Guard, went off duty after a particularly trying Sunday. On duty most of the day, they had not been released until six in the evening, and "had just lined up for their first hot meal of the day when they were sent back to duty on campus." The reason was the sit-in at Prentice Gate. Still without a decent meal, the members of Troop G finally got to bed around one o'clock Monday morning, only to be roused three hours later to relieve Company A of the 145th Infantry Regiment. No food and little sleep are not conducive to a good temper or to professional conduct, and in this case there had also been the bad experiences in the truckers' strike. The mood was one of anger and disgust with those responsible for prolonging the misery. Patience and tolerance were in short supply among the men of Troop G when they were ordered out again before sunrise.

Once again, responsibility rests with the officials—this time, the National Guard command. Del Corso left his men Sunday, not to return until after the shooting. Canterbury went with him but did come back Monday, too late, however, to change from his civilian clothes into uniform. During the short time the guardsmen had been on the campus, they had had several confrontations with demonstrators and received no apparent official reprimand for their excesses. The soldiers had seen a general throwing rocks at students. They had been allowed to chase young men and women with their bayonets as though they had been out hunting, and even managed to stick a few.

The announcement of a rally on the Commons to take place at noon on Monday was first made at the ceremonial burying of the Constitution three days earlier. Events since then had guaranteed that the turnout would exceed anything in the university's sixty years. By now a considerable number of students were aware that Governor Rhodes had not asked for an injunction prohibiting the rally and that the Matson-Frisina "special message" was therefore meaningless. There were also students who were unaware that Rhodes had been in Kent, that Matson and Frisina had issued anything, or even that a local state of civil emergency was in effect. Many students—including the "stable" ones, to use James Michener's adjective, who rarely, if ever, participated in rallies such as this—had been aroused by the National Guard's conduct to want to express, if only by their presence, a protest at the military arrogance that threatened their rights as citizens.

There was resentment, animosity, disgust, and anger on both sides this morning, but a confrontation was not inevitable. On the contrary, the return to a normal working day, with classes as usual, in accordance with President White's instructions issued on Sunday, helped restore an atmosphere of normalcy that had been absent during the weekend. It was up to Ohio officials to make sure that no clash occurred between guardsmen and students.

However, the same intransigence that had dominated past decisions at Kent State prevailed once more during an important meeting in the town at ten that morning. Present were General Canterbury and the National Guard's official legal officer, Major William R. Shrimp; Kent State officials President White and Vice President Matson; local officials Mayor LeRoy Satrom and his Safety Director, Paul Hershey; and Major Donald E. Manly of the Ohio Highway Patrol.

At first it seemed possible that reason would prevail. Canterbury, to the relief of the university representatives, expressed "his desire to withdraw the Guard." But Satrom "insisted that a dangerous situation persisted." White should then have asserted his authority and said that that might be true in the town but, as far as the campus was concerned, the students and their administrators wanted the Guard withdrawn. However, White said no such thing, and the discussion turned to how the noon rally should be handled. At this point "General Canterbury asked the university representatives whether or not it should be permitted"—which proves once and for all that there was no legal validity to the Matson-Frisina document. Matson-Frisina had said that the governor's state of emergency "prohibited" all rallies, peaceful or otherwise. If so, Canterbury would not have brought up the rally as a point of discussion. Tompkins and Anderson correctly analyze this aspect of the May 4 meeting, pointing out that both Canterbury and Major Shrimp would have known the rally could not be permitted if the state of emergency had existed, and therefore would not have "allowed university officials to participate in the decision as to whether or not the rally scheduled for noon should be prohibited."

General Canterbury insisted before the Scranton Commission that it was White who told him the rally must not be permitted, that it would be highly dangerous. President White told the commission that everyone who knew him would know that he would have requested that Canterbury not interfere with a peaceful assembly. This "contradiction" has not been investigated subsequently. Yet who decided that the rally should be dispersed is of major importance: that decision violated Constitutional rights which had not been extinguished by the local emergency law. As a direct result, four young lives were lost.

As the officials were arguing back and forth whether the rally should be permitted, it was already under way on the Commons at Kent State. According to the Scranton Commission, "some had vaguely heard that a rally would be held. Some came to protest the presence of the National Guard. Some were simply curious, or had free time because their classes had been cancelled. Some students stopped by on their way to or from lunch or class. The Commons is a crossroads between major university buildings. Many students who described themselves as 'straight,' or conservative, later attributed their presence at the rally to a desire to protest against the National Guard." By the time the meeting in Kent broke up at about 11:30, a sizable crowd had gathered around the Victory Bell, and they did so lawfully.

Between 11:30 and 11:40, General Canterbury and Lieutenant Colonel Fassinger, commander of the 2nd Squadron, 107th Armored Cavalry, arrived on the Commons. President White went off to have lunch at the Brown Derby restaurant. Canterbury's initial reaction on seeing the assembled students was to do nothing, which only deepens the mystery of who ordered the rally dispersed. Considerable emphasis has been placed on the legality of the rally: as Michener observed, "the validity of subsequent indictments and punishment" depends upon a judicial determination of this question. Both the federal government and the state of Ohio have stubbornly refused to allow the judiciary to make such a determination, so we are left with a few facts from which conclusions can be drawn. In Michener's opinion, the rally "was certainly not illegal in civil law," because Canterbury's decision to act upon the Matson-Frisina decree was without lawful authorization. The National Guard, Michener points out, "was acting solely on the verbal assurance of the Governor, which would have to be interpreted as 'law by personal decree.' This is legal in no American state." Mindful of Mayor Satrom's state of civil emergency, which permitted peaceful assembly and demonstration on the campus, the students conducted themselves peacefully and made sure the Guard would have no excuse to repeat their performance of the night before. That the rally was indeed peaceful has been confirmed by both the Justice Department and the Scranton Commission. (See photo 2.)

At 11:45 many classes ended and more students drifted into the area on their way to other classes, to lunch, or to their rooms. In doing so, they swelled the now considerable crowd to two thousand or three thousand in all. At about 11:50 Canterbury apparently undertook to disperse the peaceful assembly. He directed that the students be informed of his intentions. With the assistance of a bullhorn, the crowd was ordered to leave. The order was greeted with jeers and insults by those who could hear it; many did not. The distance between the bullhorn and the students was too great, so a jeep was sent out from the National Guard line at the foot of the Commons. The vehicle drove up fairly close to the assembled students. "Attention! This is an order. Disperse immediately. This is an order. Leave this area immediately. This is an order. Disperse." (See photo 6.)

Whose order? By what authority? Why should the students disperse? What were they doing to warrant Canterbury's arbitrary violation of their Constitutional rights? The Scranton Commission reported that many students "were legitimately in the area as they went to and from class," but in fact *all* students were legitimately in the area, be they demonstrators, observers, bystanders, or passers-by. "Only when the Guard attempted to disperse the rally," the commission concluded, "did some students react violently." Is it realistic to condemn students who reacted after the gassing and bayoneting of that Sunday night? The students were lawfully assembled and the National Guard was unlawfully ordering them to disperse.

The jeep was subjected to thrown rocks, and its occupants to catcalls and obscenities. Few of the missiles, Michener says, reached the army vehicle, and "none appear to have struck any of the four passengers." The man announcing General Canterbury's order to disperse was Kent State policeman Harold E. Rice. When it became obvious to Canterbury that the students were not going to obey, he sent Major Jones out to recall the jeep to the National Guard position close by the ruins of the ROTC building.

At 11:55 guardsmen were selected to take part in carrying out the dispersal order and the men chosen were ordered to "lock and load" their weapons. This calls for the guardsmen to insert clips of ammunition into their guns and place one round in the chamber ready for firing. It was at this moment that someone sought out Canterbury and told him, "You must not march against the students." As the crowd was still relatively peaceful, this was sound advice. But, as reported by Michener, the general set the tone for what was to follow by replying, "These students are going to have to find out what law and order is all about." Michener suggests that the unknown person who approached Canterbury in a last-minute effort to avert the confrontation may have been a member of the faculty.

On Sunday it had been Portage County Prosecutor Kane trying to convince Governor Rhodes to close down Kent State for a cooling-off period. On Monday it was "someone" trying to avert potential disaster at the brink. But no one was listening. The kids had to be shown what law and order is all about.

Almost exactly at noon, the first tear-gas canister was fired at the crowd and the guardsmen stepped off in a skirmish line toward the students. The Scranton Commission reports: "The May 4 rally began as a peaceful assembly on the Commons—the traditional site of student assemblies. Even if the Guard had authority to prohibit a peaceful gathering—a question that is at least debatable—the decision to disperse the noon rally was a serious error."

The advance of the National Guard was directed by three senior officers: Brigadier General Canterbury, Lieutenant Colonel Fassinger, and Major Jones. Men from three units constituted the total force: Companies A and C of the 145th Infantry Regiment and Troop G of the 107th Armored Cavalry. Company A, under the immediate command of Captain John E. Martin, took the right flank. Company C, under Captain Ronald Snyder, was assigned the left flank. Troop G, commanded by Captain Raymond Srp, had the center. Four lieutenants completed the group of officers: Dwight Kline and Howard Fallon of Company A, William Herthneck of Company C, and Alexander Stevenson of Troop G. Ten officers and 103 enlisted men in all.

As the force moved out, they were all wearing gas masks except the three senior officers. Some carried .45 pistols, most carried M-1 rifles, and a few carried shotguns loaded with birdshot and buckshot. Major Jones also carried a .22 Beretta pistol. Company C, the Justice Department says, was instructed to remember that "if any firing was to be done, it would be done by one man firing in the air (presumably on the order of the officer in charge)." With respect to the two units which eventually *did* fire their weapons, the Justice Department says only that "it is not known whether any instructions concerning the firing of weapons were given to either Company A or Troop G."

The Guard's mission, Canterbury later testified before the Scranton Commission, was to disperse the crowd on the Commons. To accomplish this, he decided on a pincer movement directed at the east and west ends of Taylor Hall. Company A and Troop G would head for the west corner, where Blanket Hill runs up between Taylor and Johnson halls, while Company C made for the east corner and the area between Taylor and Prentice halls. (See map.)

At 12.02, as the line of advancing guardsmen neared the Victory Bell, Captain Snyder detached his force from the main body and headed for his objective. A considerable amount of tear gas had been fired at the crowd, but most of it was ineffective because of the wind. Some of the students started cursing the guardsmen, shouting obscenities at them, while many more took up anti-war chants. A few threw rocks and stones, but, as Michener reports, "the distances between the mass of students and the Guards were later stepped off by expert judges, who concluded that students would have required good right arms like Mickey Mantle's to have reached the Guardsmen even with

34

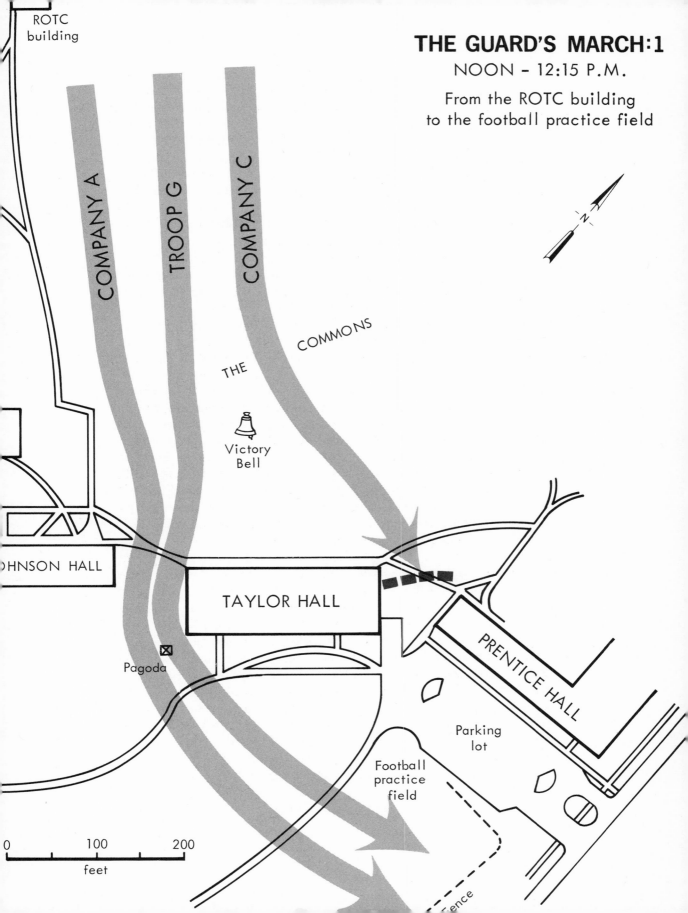

small stones." Occasionally, however, a student ran toward the advancing guardsmen to throw his missile. Contrary to the Ohio National Guard's claim that over fifty of their men were injured on May 4, the Justice Department summary of the FBI investigation found that "only one Guardsman, Lawrence Shafer, was injured on May 4, 1970, seriously enough to require any kind of medical treatment." Shafer sustained the injury on the football practice field ten to fifteen minutes before the shooting. "His arm, which was badly bruised, was put in a sling," the Justice Department says, "and he was given medication for pain"—after the fatal volley was fired. Shafer took part in the shooting, and the injury did not prevent him, according to the FBI, from deliberately aiming at and shooting down Joseph Lewis.

With the advance of the Guard and the firing of more tear gas, the participants in the rally began to drift back up Blanket Hill toward the area between Taylor and Johnson halls. Some stood their ground for a while, but memories of the previous night's bayoneting were sufficiently fresh in many minds to discourage any desire for face-to-face confrontations. At the Victory Bell, Captain Snyder led Company C off to the left. The main body under Canterbury and Fassinger continued up Blanket Hill in pursuit of the fleeing students. In photograph 14, Company C is in the foreground, heading toward the eastern end of Taylor Hall, background left. In right center is the Victory Bell, where the rally began. At the extreme right is Major Jones running to catch up with Company C, and in the background can be seen Troop G and Company A on their ascent of Blanket Hill. The significance of this photograph by John Filo, one which was not included in the Scranton Commission's report, is that it shows clearly that the sole purpose of the Guard's advance has been accomplished: the Commons has been cleared and the noon rally dispersed.

As the main force under Canterbury reached the western end of Taylor Hall, a few students lingered at the crest of Blanket Hill to shout obscenities at the men of Troop G, who, since the departure of Company C, now held the extreme left flank of the line with Company A strung out to the right. Among the students was Allison Krause.

In his study of Kent State, James Michener notes the obscenities shouted at the guardsmen and observes that the obscenities, "especially when launched by coeds," were "worse, in a way, than the missiles" which could physically injure. "Girls were particularly abusive," he says, "using the foulest language"; others "called them less explosive but equally hurtful names: 'toy soldiers, murderers, weekend warriors, fascists.' " Riot-control training in both civilian law enforcement and the National Guard stresses the need to ignore verbal abuse. Those proffering abuse are venting their anger or childishly aping others, or deliberately seeking to arouse a reaction. Professionalism collapses once men trained in civil-disturbance control allow themselves to be incited by obscenities. Of the five guardsmen of Troop G identified by the Justice Department as having admitted firing into the crowd or at a specific student, four of them had had sixty hours of riot-control training, and the fifth, James Pierce, "an unknown, but probably substantial, number of hours of riot-control training." Three of these guardsmen had earlier participated in three riots, one of them in two riots, and Pierce, a Kent State student at the time, in one. "None are novices," the Justice Department dryly comments.

Michener reports that Captain Snyder of Company C, leading his men through the trees toward the northeast corner of Taylor Hall, encountered "a bushy-haired young man" who threw a handful of stones at Snyder. The captain reportedly turned his back, then "spun around and brought his baton down across the boy's shoulders with such force as to snap off the tip of the baton." Michener then says the young man "reached in his pocket and brought forth . . . a brass knuckle. Snyder hit him again. He dropped the piece of metal and dashed back up the hill." This was the first known face-to-face clash of the day between a civilian and a guardsman. Three photographs, 18, 19, and 20, appear to have captured the incident. The most significant of the three pictures is 20, in which three guardsmen are seen aiming their M-1 rifles at an undisclosed target. This photograph was taken at approximately 12:05, so this constitutes the first filmed incident in which guardsmen aim their weapons at students. The second took place on the practice field about ten minutes later, when members of Troop G aimed their rifles at students in the Prentice Hall parking lot. The third recorded time when the soldiers aimed their weapons was at 12:24 P.M., when they fired. These photographs were not included in the Scranton Commission report. Whether the guardsman with the bullhorn is actually Captain Snyder or not, the photographs do show that Company C was the first of the three units to experience personal contact with demonstrators and the first to threaten the students with gunfire.

As the main Guard force attained the crest of Blanket Hill, the students poured around the southwest corner of Taylor Hall. Photograph 17, taken from the terrace of that building, is further confirmation that the students were leaving the Commons and few were harassing the Guard.

For reasons that are still unclear, General Canterbury did not halt his men at this point and consolidate his position. With Troop G and Company A sealing off the Blanket Hill route to the Commons between Taylor and Johnson halls and Company C sealing off the area between Taylor and Prentice halls which also led to the Commons, Canterbury would have been able to assess the situation and his men would have held a tenable position. Instead, he ordered the men to continue forward down the slope in front of Taylor Hall and on to the football practice field. Thus he exposed the guardsmen to virtual encirclement by students, since the football field has a long, six-foot-high chain-link fence running the entire length of its eastern end and swinging around at the northern end, where a baseball diamond is located. "It was inconceivable," says Michener, "that soldiers would march with their eyes open into such a trap." But they did, and Canterbury was responsible. The Scranton Commission simply concluded that the "Guard's decision to march through the crowd for hundreds of yards up and down a hill was highly questionable."

Once on the football practice field, the guardsmen could go no farther and came to a halt. The crowd had fanned out into the Prentice Hall parking lot, along the slope in front of Taylor Hall, and onto the terrace, with small groups along the southern end of the field. The Guard force consisted of seventy-five men: a general, a lieutenant colonel, two captains, three lieutenants, and sixty-eight men, seventeen of whom were sergeants. Two men from Company C had tagged along with Company A. Later they would fire their weapons and thereby become the only members of this unit known to have fired on May 4. Both claimed they did not fire at the students.

When the guardsmen came to a dead end, it was the men of Troop G who were closest to the students in the Prentice Hall parking lot a good hundred feet or more away. In the parking lot were several students who had made themselves conspicuous to some of the guardsmen by consistent and persistent harassment ever since the troops first stepped off from the ruins of the ROTC building. Among these students were Allison Krause, Jeffrey Miller, and Alan Canfora. With the Guard on the practice field, Allison continued her verbal abuse, Jeff threw back a tear-gas canister from some hundred and fifty feet, and Alan waved a black flag. Also during this time, Dean Kahler, Thomas Grace, and Robert Stamps harassed the guardsmen. In less than fifteen minutes, all six would be shot, two fatally.

Two incidents during the National Guard's ten-minute stay on the practice field became highly significant after the shooting. The first underscores the key point made by the Justice Department's summary of the FBI investigation, and later by Attorney General John Mitchell, that at no time were the lives of the guardsmen in serious danger. Major Harry Jones had accompanied Captain Snyder and Company C to secure the eastern end of Taylor Hall. Canterbury's decision to continue down to the practice field put Company C behind the crowd, facing the troops clustered on the field. When Jones realized that there was some kind of command confusion on the football field, the Justice Department reports, the major "walked through the crowd to find out if General Canterbury wanted assistance." Michener says that Jones rejoined the main force by "elbowing his way through the crowd of students." If the demonstrators were as dangerous as Canterbury claimed after the killings, could a solitary officer have elbowed his way through them without some kind of incident? Yet that is exactly what happened. With Jones's arrival on the field, the main force now consisted of seventy-six men, eight of them officers.

The second filmed incident of the soldiers aiming at the students foreshadowed what was to happen in a few minutes during the Guard's return march back to the Commons. The men of Troop G, the Justice Department reports, "were ordered to kneel and aim their weapons at the students in the parking lot south of Prentice Hall. They did so, but did not fire. One person, however, probably an officer, at this point did fire a pistol in the air. No guardsman admits firing this shot."

Joe Eszterhas and Michael Roberts, reporting in the May 13, 1970, edition of the Cleveland *Plain Dealer,* said that three people saw a "short officer" fire a .45 pistol with his left hand while the guardsmen were on the football practice field. The witnesses were identified as Professor Richard Schreiber, Sharon Keene, and Patrick Carr. Schreiber told Dr. Carl Moore of Kent State's speech department that the weapon fired by the guardsman on the practice field was definitely not a revolver but a .45 automatic.

By any yardstick, it would seem important that the identity of this guardsman be established and the reason for his action determined. The FBI says he fired. In so doing, he could easily have triggered the kind of volley that would occur shortly from the vantage point of the Pagoda with its elevation of almost twenty feet above the parking lot. When the shooting did take place, the firing would be directed into the parking lot into which the men of Troop G were now aiming their M-1 rifles, and it would be the men of Troop G who would start the shooting.

Was the shot fired on the football practice field a signal to shoot? If it was, why did the guardsmen ignore the cue? If it was not a signal, why did the guardsman fire, by whose authority did he do so, and why has no guardsman admitted firing this shot if there is nothing to conceal from investigators? Several photographs taken at the time the men of Troop G were kneeling and aiming at the students in the parking lot show General Canterbury with his back to the guardsmen, engrossed in some papers. Obviously, the general considered the student threat to his men insignificant at this time.

When the men of Troop G knelt and aimed their weapons, the harassment by the crowd, primarily vocal, increased sharply. The Justice Department and the Scranton Commission both concluded that at this moment the harassment reached its peak for the entire twenty-four minutes of the confrontation. The circus atmosphere which had developed on the commons when students started hurling tear-gas canisters back at the guardsmen (photos 11, 15) resumed on the practice field (photos 29, 35).

39

Of the kneeling and aiming, Michener says only that "it appears that they must have been ordered by some officer to assume this frightening and provocative position." He goes on to recognize the gravity of it by noting that "if a further command had been given at this moment, students on the parking lot would have been mowed down, but no such command was uttered." Though he makes no reference to the Justice Department's statement that someone did fire on the football field, Michener describes in detail witnesses' accounts of seeing a guardsman fire his .45 pistol. "I happened to have this one Guard in my glasses (7×35 Bushnell binoculars), and I saw him raise his revolver and bang away," one witness told Michener. "There can be no question but that he fired the first round of the day." Michener apparently did not attach too much significance to who this guardsman was and why he fired. Yet the answers to those questions might be of immense value.

What happened when the guardsmen were on the practice field is as important as what happened later. For a good six minutes the troops were immobile and therefore easier targets for both missiles and obscenities. As has been mentioned, official investigations concluded that it was now that the students' harassment of the Guard was at its worst. However, the testimony of a number of witnesses refutes this conclusion, and several photographs support that testimony. The Justice Department says the "number of rock throwers at this time is not known and the estimates range between 10 and 50." The Department expresses the belief "that the rock throwing reached its peak at this time" and reports that four guardsmen "claim they were hit with rocks at this time." The Scranton Commission reports that the crowd "on the parking lot was unruly and threw many missiles at guardsmen on the football field. It was at this point that the shower of stones apparently became heaviest." Guardsmen responded with tear gas and, in at least one instance (photo 23), with a rock. General Del Corso had already demonstrated to the men how to throw rocks "at those bastards." Witnesses who did not participate in this harassment are highly inconsistent in their estimates of how many students were actually throwing missiles at the guardsmen and what effect they were having in the Guard ranks.

Harold Walker told James Michener: "It's true that a few kids, maybe ten, ran inside the baseball fence to throw rocks and junk at the Guardsmen, but very little reached them." Joseph Carter told Eszterhas and Roberts he saw "about fifteen students throw rocks" at the guardsmen and that most of them did so from distances of from 80 to 125 feet. Michael Erwin told them that "twenty-five to thirty people were throwing rocks," whereas John Barilla "saw four or five." The Justice Department's figure of "10 to 50" just about covers the range of estimates. Photographs, however, are somewhat more reliable, and

24 and 25 (both included in the Scranton Commission report) confirm that there were relatively few students in the parking lot, compared to the number in front of Taylor Hall. It is photograph 26, however, which is the most convincing and the one that deeply impressed Michener when he saw it. The men of Troop G are aiming their weapons at a few students who are 150 to 200 feet from them. One explanation is that the students who were harassing the guardsmen had already drawn attention to themselves by running up near or to the fence and throwing missiles, as Jeff Miller and Dean Kahler did, or shouting obscenities, like Allison Krause, or waving black flags, like Alan Canfora, and then retreating back toward the wall of Prentice Hall. The guardsmen could still see the flags, and it is not impossible that they could still see Jeff and Allison too, even though they were two hundred feet away. Photograph 27, taken with a telephoto lens by Howard Ruffner, covers the distance seen in 26 from the front wheel of the parked car at the extreme right center, over to the grass island at the extreme lower left, and in it thirteen students can be counted, one with a black flag. Again this bears out the witnesses who insisted that at the most there were no more than fifteen students in the parking lot who kept up word- or rock-throwing harassment of the guardsmen.

When Lieutenant Colonel Fassinger passed on the order to regroup back at the ruins of the ROTC, it was 12:18 in the afternoon. During the next couple of minutes, as the guardsmen began forming into a V-shaped skirmish line for the return march, a third incident occurred on the football field, and again it involved Troop G. A number of witnesses described it as a "huddle," and Michener puts the crucial question to the reader in these words: "When the Guard went into their huddle on the practice field, was an order given that they should fire when they reached the pagoda?" Michener had no answer: "There is at present no evidence, and there may never be, for on this point no Guardsman will now allow himself to be interrogated." One can do no more than speculate, but there are strong indications that such evidence exists, not least of which is the fact that Michener leans toward the belief that a decision was made on the practice field to punish the students. "It seems likely," he wrote, "that on the football field, when the students were being obnoxious and stones were drifting in, that some of the troops agreed among themselves, 'We've taken about enough of this crap. If they don't stop pretty soon we're going to let them have it.' It was in this mood that they retreated up the hill—hot, dusty, sweating, and cut off from the rational world by their gas masks."

Having offered the most logical explanation for what happened—why most of the men in Troop G suddenly opened fire—Michener later does a complete about-face and says: "It was an accident,

41

deplorable and tragic," and "There was death, but not murder." If some of Troop G agreed among themselves to shoot, then it was no accident. It was, as James Ahern, a member of the Scranton Commission, said, simply a question of murder or manslaughter.

Neither the Scranton Commission nor the Justice Department mentions the so-called huddle, but something took place among Troop G just before the Guard's departure from the football field that conveyed the impression of a huddle. Photograph 37 has captured what these witnesses saw. The contrast between the men in Troop G bunched up, with some of them walking in different directions, and the men in Company A is significant, if not conclusive. In the foreground can be seen one of the black flags that was waved at the guardsmen—waved and nothing more, but persistently, throughout the Guard's march around campus.

What happened on the practice field is inseparable from what happened a few minutes later at the Pagoda. The Justice Department summary of the FBI investigation points to the possibility that there was indeed, as Michener put it, "some kind of rough verbal agreement" among the men of Troop G "when they clustered on the practice field." The summary admits that the FBI could find no satisfactory explanation for the fact that most of Troop G suddenly spun around and opened fire on students in the parking lot. In other words, we are left with the clear possibility that a decision was reached among these men to shoot at the students. Five members of Troop G long ago admitted to the FBI that they did indeed shoot "into the crowd," but they have never been called upon to explain why or be subjected to cross examination. And their original excuses have been dismissed by Attorney General Mitchell and refuted by the photographic record.

The next sequence of photographs spans the return march of the guardsmen from the football field to the Pagoda, the point where the shooting took place. We still do not *know* whether or not a few guardsmen had conspired during those few minutes when they were immobile on the football practice field, compelled, by the folly of their commanders, to endure harassment by a handful of students in the parking lot and the particularly vocal abuse from many among the large crowd spread out in front of Taylor Hall. Photographs do not provide us with the answer, but they show that the men of Troop G, during this retreat from the Guard's impossible position on the practice field, evinced a continual interest in, and observation of, the students in the parking lot, apparently to the exclusion of students much closer to them and visible in these pictures. Why?

Like the Justice Department, the Scranton Commission, and Michener, we can only speculate. In photographs 38 through 42 we see Troop G and Company A commencing their return to the Commons. The slower departure by members of Troop G is quite apparent in photos 39 and 40, but what is most striking is that in these two photographs the men of Troop G stand out in stark contrast to the men in Company A, who are proceeding forthrightly forward. Except for a few, the men of Company A are looking ahead and marching determinedly forward, not straggling and looking back at the parking lot. In photograph 39, six members of Troop G are looking back toward the parking lot.

Apologists for the Ohio National Guard contend that Troop G's surveillance of the parking lot is explained away by the argument that they were the closest guardsmen to that trouble spot and therefore it was their responsibility to protect the right flank by keeping a careful eye on the students who had persistently harassed them while they were on the football field. This is a logical and reasonable explanation, except for two facts which at the least cast some doubt on its validity. First of all, it seems odd that the men in Company A on the extreme right flank of that unit's line should place such confidence in the men of Troop G's ability to warn them of oncoming missiles that they can generally ignore the parking lot. Secondly, it seems odd that as the two units start to climb the slope in front of Taylor Hall some men of Troop G apparently feel no danger from students quite close to them but keep up their surveillance of the parking lot, which is gradually getting farther away from them as they climb the hill to the Pagoda. In photograph 42, for example, there appear to be more men in Troop G looking back at the eastern end of the parking lot, now two hundred feet away, than are observing the students in the foreground of the picture.

Another notable aspect of these photographs is the students who appear in them. In photograph 39 we see a student with a black flag, and in 42 we see a couple, the young man carrying a folder, and three students also looking toward the football field rather than at the guardsmen. There is an element of unreality in many of these photographs in light of what was going to happen. It is shatteringly obvious that the danger to the lives of the guardsmen was absolutely minimal.

This sense of unreality is even sharper in photographs 43 and 44. The guardsmen are proceeding up the slope toward the Pagoda, some men in Troop G still keeping a close watch on the receding parking lot and on the northern end of the football practice field. As they do so, students Miller, Krause, Kahler, Canfora, Grace, and Stamps are still in this very area. The few students in these two pictures are close to the guardsmen but obviously passive. In photograph 43, however, we see, for the first time, a guardsman with a .45 pistol in his *left* hand. The man directly in front of him with a .45 in his right hand appeared in earlier photographs with gun drawn when the Guard started out from the football field. The significance of the man with a .45 in his

43

left hand does not become apparent until the shooting, at which time such a guardsman appears in the forefront of the line, aiming and, apparently, firing his .45 pistol in the direction of the parking lot.

In photograph 45 we see a view from another angle of the scene in 43. The student standing still, with a folder in his right hand, appears in both pictures. The Justice Department and the Scranton Commission both drew attention to the fact that there were no students impeding the course the guardsmen were embarked on and that they could have returned to the Commons without further incident. Photographs 46 and 47 provide two different views of the guardsmen approaching the Pagoda. Photograph 46 clearly bears out the official findings, but it does not show what might be in front of Company A, who are seen to the left of the lamppost. In photograph 47 we see the situation from behind Company A, and again it is quite apparent that nothing impedes their march back to the ruins of the ROTC.

To return to photograph 46, we see once again that curious bunching of Troop G in a sort of knot, with quite a few of the men looking back into the very area into which they are shortly going to be shooting. If a decision was made by some members of Troop G to shoot, then their preoccupation with students in the parking lot is explained.

Photographs 48 and 49, the last before the guardsmen turn, speak for themselves. In 48, Troop G has just crossed the last path before the Pagoda. This picture was taken by Richard C. Harris, Jr., who was at the eastern end of the parking lot into which the shooting is going to be directed. It clearly establishes that there were no students impeding the Guard's forward progress to the Commons. It also disproves General Canterbury's claim that a "mob" was bearing down on the guardsmen that would become so "threatening" that the soldiers had to shoot for their lives. In fact, the students both in the parking lot and in front of Taylor Hall are generally passive, not aggressive. Less than ten seconds after this photograph was taken, the guardsmen in the picture will wheel around and shoot toward the cameraman. At this moment Allison Krause is near the station wagon in the center of the photograph, Jeff Miller is to the left of that vehicle, Sandy Scheuer is off to the extreme left walking toward the cameraman's position, and Bill Schroeder is near Sandy. The picture adequately conveys the distance of three hundred feet or more between the guardsmen and the students in the parking lot.

In photograph 49 the guardsmen are about to crest the hill and commence their descent back to ROTC. The metal sculpture, at the extreme right, is a hundred feet from the Pagoda. It would appear that the reason why none of the students in the foreground was wounded or killed by the first rounds is that the guardsmen were aiming over their heads at the parking lot. The combination of distance and elevation seen in photograph 48 spared them. By the time the volley ended, two students—John Cleary, beside the sculpture, and Joseph Lewis, beyond him—had been shot. What happened after this photo was taken is officially termed "unclear." This reflects a reluctance to tackle the obvious. There were scores of witnesses, and the only conflict in their testimony revolves around such questions as whether there were one or two shots, whether there was a signal, whether it was an officer or a sergeant who gave the signal, and whether he was wearing a gas mask or not. On the key question of whether there was a reason for the soldiers suddenly to start shooting, the witnesses are almost all agreed: there was none. On the equally important question whether the first shot, from a small-caliber weapon, preceded or followed the sudden turn, there is less certainty on the part of those who were watching the guardsmen. Six of the witnesses testified before the Kent State Commission convened by President White in the aftermath of the killings:

"I don't think the Guard panicked. It seemed too orderly, and they fired as though on command."

"It is my observation that it was completely impossible for that number of men to act spontaneously, yet in such perfect unison; there simply had to be an order from someone, and it would appear that someone had chosen in advance a commanding point to make their stand."

"Suddenly, as if on command, although I did not hear one, the National Guard turned toward the crowd who had moved onto the practice field and into the parking lot."

"I saw a guardsman with a side arm draw from his holster, aiming into the crowd, he fired. At the same time, simultaneously with, and no pause between this, the rest of the guardsmen also fired."

"As [the Guard] crested the hill, they stopped, they turned, and at this time I saw a man withdraw a side arm from his holster, aim it at the crowd, and fire into the crowd. With this firing, or at the same time, I saw there were other guardsmen with rifles that shot into the crowd."

"It appeared that there was someone in command since the troops, immediately prior to the shooting, did turn and consolidate into a more consolidated line, more or less simultaneously."

A number of witnesses testified to seeing a guardsman draw a pistol, raise it in the air, then lower and fire it in the direction of the practice field and the parking lot. Some of these witnesses describe the guardsman as an officer.

Howard Ruffner's photograph, 50, was taken just after the completion of what James Michener described as "that sudden and dramatic turn of 135° before firing." It was indeed sudden and without reason, unless, of course, this is what they planned to do when they reached this "commanding point to make their stand." Careful study of the picture reveals only one man with a .45 pistol in a posture of bringing

45

down his left arm to shoot or, possibly, in recoil after having fired. General Canterbury, seen in the background peering over his right shoulder, testified under oath to the Scranton Commission that at this moment a "mob" of students was charging the Guard and had come to "within four and five yards" of his men. It would appear from the photograph that Canterbury was completely in the dark about why the guardsmen were shooting. It is equally obvious that four students were killed at distances which make a cruel mockery of the Guard's claims of self-defense.

Donald MacKenzie, one of the students shot by the guardsmen, told Eszterhas and Roberts that " 'one of the guardsmen turned and fired, and then I heard the volley.' As the guardsmen turned, they rushed a few steps back up the knoll, firing, led by a guardsman with a .45 pistol." This guardsman, with the .45 weapon, appears again in photograph 52 in a position consistent with his having "led" the men back a few steps toward the parking lot into which they were shooting. He is out front in a posture that strongly indicates that he is shooting. One witness who was on the Taylor Hall terrace told me she was watching the guardsman with the .45 and saw his arm come down, saw smoke come from his gun and his arm jerk upward in recoil. She saw him do this more than once. It was not until May 24, 1970, that this particular guardsman was identified by the Akron *Beacon Journal* as First Sergeant Myron C. Pryor, senior noncommissioned officer of Troop G. The *Beacon Journal* reported:

John A. Darnell, a senior journalism student, standing on the Taylor veranda with a 15-year-old Japanese-made camera around his neck, took three photographs during the firing. One [52] would appear on two pages of *Life* magazine—nine guardsmen with rifles leveled. A left-handed soldier, gripping a .45, stood crouched a foot or two ahead. It appears as if he is leading the squad. Eventually the FBI would believe it knew the identity of the man with the .45.

His name is Mike Pryor. He is a career Army man, forty-ish, bald, and the first sergeant for the 145th [sic]. He lives on a tree-shaded residential street close to downtown Akron with his wife and two frisky dogs. His wife was terrified when she heard a false report over the radio that two guardsmen had been killed.

Pryor is left-handed. Normally, though, he shoots with his right hand. Before the ascent to Blanket Hill, he had burned his right hand. To the FBI he acknowledged he was on the hill armed with a .45. He recalls drawing the weapon when the firing began. He said the man in the *Life* photograph "could be" him. He said he doesn't believe it is. He said he did not fire.

The FBI, which now has the weapon, believes he is correct. Although it appears in the photograph that the weapon is in recoil position, gun experts point out that the shooter's arm is stiff. If fired, the recoil would jerk the arm upwards. Conceivably, however, he could have had the gun aimed to the ground and had it jerk upward upon discharge.

The FBI believes a more likely explanation is that the weapon is either

46

in "lock and load" position or jammed. To a reporter, First Sergeant Pryor denied that he was on the hill. "I've been in battle before," he said, "and couldn't remember what happened five minutes afterwards."

It is difficult to understand why the *Beacon Journal* analyzed the sergeant's stiff arm as appearing to be in "recoil position." This could be the case in photograph 51 but not in 52. The experts, of course, are right. The stiff arm suggests he is about to fire rather than that he has already fired. But he denies ever firing his .45 at Kent State on May 4, 1970, and in September 1971 in fact claimed that his pistol contained "an empty magazine." If this is true, then the FBI assessment is incorrect. With an empty magazine, the gun could not be in "lock and load" position, nor could it be "jammed." A great deal hinges upon these two photographs and what Sergeant Pryor is doing in them.

The mystery surrounding this particular guardsman is deepened further by the Justice Department in its summary of the FBI investigation. In speculating on possible explanations for the shooting, the Department suggests "that the members of Troop G observed their top noncommissioned officer, Sergeant Pryor, turn and point his weapon at the crowd and followed his example." The summary goes on to report that "Sergeant Pryor admits that he was pointing his weapon at the students prior to the shooting but claims he was loading it and denies he fired." The Justice Department says: "The FBI does not believe he fired." Why this agency, renowned for its ballistics expertise, should be unable to state categorically whether or not the .45 was fired is difficult to understand. All weapons that had been issued to the guardsmen involved in the shooting were examined by the FBI. From that examination the Justice Department was able to charge that, of the forty-seven guardsmen who claimed they did not fire, "at least two and possibly more Guardsmen are lying concerning this fact." The Department identifies one of the two men as SP/4 William F. Herschler of Company A, on the basis of a statement by Sergeant Mathew J. McManus to the FBI that he saw Herschler empty "his entire clip of eight rounds into the crowd—firing semi-automatically." As for the other guardsman alleged to have lied, the Justice Department simply says: "In addition to Herschler, at least one person who has not admitted firing his weapon, did so. The FBI is currently in possession of four spent .45 cartridges which came from a weapon not belonging to any person who admitted he fired.

The Scranton Commission reports that "two men fired pistols: one said he fired two shots into the crowd and the other said he fired three shots into the air." The Justice Department identified the guardsman who fired two shots into the crowd with his .45 as Staff Sergeant Barry Morris of Troop G. They also report that SP/4 James D. McGee, who carried an M-1 rifle and admitted firing it three times—"twice over the heads of the crowd"—told the FBI that he "saw one soldier from Company A fire four or five rounds from a .45 and saw a sergeant from Troop G also fire a .45 into the crowd." The latter could have been Sergeant Morris. The problem, and it is one that the Justice Department recognized, is how many guardsmen in Troop G actually did fire. Twelve admitted doing so to federal agents, but only five admitted shooting into the crowd or at a specific student. However, in photograph 52 there are at least nine guardsmen who are aiming and shooting in the direction of the students, and the Ohio National Guard roster of guardsmen who fired weapons on May 4, 1970, shows that ten of the sixteen men in Troop G fired. The only members listed by the Guard as not having fired are First Sergeant Pryor, Staff Sergeant Rudy E. Morris, Sergeant Lawrence Shafer, SP/4 John R. Baclawski, PFC Michael D. McCoy, and PFC Paul R. McCoy. Troop G's officers, Captain Srp and Lieutenant Stevenson, are also listed as not having fired. As the Justice Department said, "at least two and possibly more Guardsmen are lying" in claiming that they did not fire.

General Canterbury's testimony to the Scranton Commission constituted the Ohio National Guard's sole explanation for the shooting:

> As the troop formation reached the area of the Pagoda near Taylor Hall [refer to photo 48], the mob located on the right flank in front of Taylor Hall and in the Prentice Hall parking lot charged our right flank, throwing rocks, yelling obscenities and threats, "Kill the pigs," "Stick the pigs." The attitude of the crowd at this point was menacing and vicious. The troops were hit by rocks. I saw Major Jones hit in the stomach by a large brick, a guardsman to the right and rear of my position was hit by a large rock and fell to the ground. During this movement, practically all of the guardsmen were hit by missiles of various kinds. Guardsmen on the right flank were in serious danger of bodily harm and death as the mob continued to charge. I felt that, in view of the extreme danger to the troops at this point, that they were justified in firing.

The Scranton Commission notes that Canterbury "also testified that the closest students were within four to five yards of the Guard."

The general's description of what happened just before the shooting is simply contrary to the facts. There was no mob, there was no charge, and few, if any, guardsmen were hit by rocks just before the gunfire. Photographs prove this beyond doubt. Even the cautious Scranton Commission was moved to observe: "In the direction the Guard fired, however, photographs show an open space in front of the Guardsmen of at least 20 yards. To their side, the nearest student, one of several on the terrace of Taylor Hall, was at least 15 yards away. The nearest person wounded, Joseph Lewis, Jr., who was 20 yards away, said there was no one between him and the Guard. The closest person killed, Jeffrey Glenn Miller, was at least 85 yards away." In photograph 53 we see the moment when the men of Troop G have completed their turn and have just started to shoot. No one on the terrace of Taylor Hall was shot, even though that was the closest "crowd" to the guardsmen, because none of the soldiers was shooting anywhere but between the metal sculpture on their left and two trees on their right. In photograph 54, taken after Kent State was closed down following the killings, we see where that front line of guardsmen stood, what they were shooting at, and why no student on the terrace was shot despite the fact that scores of students were gathered there, the closest about forty-five feet from the near corner railing, where guardsmen are seen in photos 51 and 52 aiming over the top of the rail. Between the metal sculpture left of center and the two pine trees is the Prentice Hall parking lot and the northern edge of the football practice field where the guardsmen were immobile for some time before they marched up to the Pagoda, wheeled around, and fired back down and into the parking lot. Only two of the thirteen students shot were not between the two points through which the gunfire of those shooting "into the crowd" was aimed. One was Joseph Lewis, who was standing just on the other side of the path, center, leading up to the terrace. His position was very close, though: he was just to the right of the lamppost. The other was James Russell, who was 375 feet away from the Pagoda and off to the extreme right. The FBI reports that he was struck by falling buckshot from the shotgun blast fired into the air by SP/4 Leon H. Smith of Company A.

Once again, the distance from the Pagoda to the parking lot is evident and speaks for itself. The two parked jeeps just to the right of the sculpture are 250 feet away from the firing line. The students killed all fell beyond that distance. Yet Canterbury would have us believe the guardsmen were "in serious danger of bodily harm and death" and that the guardsmen "were justified in firing." Photograph 53 shows Joseph Lewis standing still and, as the Justice Department reports, doing no more than giving the Guard an upraised finger. For this he was deliberately shot down, once in the leg and again, seriously, in the groin.

It is photograph 53 which gives the lie to General Canterbury's statement that the "charging mob" came to within four or five yards of his men just before the shooting. As has been noted, the shooting had just started when this picture was taken, and in the direction the Guard is firing only three persons can be seen: Lewis seventy feet away from the guardsmen; behind him, someone ducking and running for the railing, about eighty-five feet away; and at the extreme left, the third person facing the guardsmen is over ninety feet away. These three students evidently comprise Canterbury's "mob" that "continued to charge" to twelve to fifteen feet from his men and posed such "extreme danger to the troops . . . that they were justified in firing."

With this photograph in mind, the statements of some of the

49

guardsmen of Troop G who admitted to the FBI that they shot into the crowd or at specific students are as interesting as General Canterbury's testimony. "SP/4 James Pierce, a Kent State student, claims that the crowd was within ten feet of the National Guardsmen. He then fired four shots—one into the air; one at a male ten feet away with his arm drawn back and a rock in his hand (this male fell and appeared to get hit again); he then turned to his right and fired into the crowd; he turned back to his left and fired at a large Negro male about to throw a rock at him." In photograph 53 we can see at least ninety feet of space between the guardsmen and the extreme left of the picture. The shooting has only just commenced, and an 8mm. film taken by Chris Abell shows that at the first burst of smoke the students begin running *away* from the guardsmen but the guardsmen continue shooting for thirteen seconds. Because of the students on the terrace in photograph 53, it is not possible to see whether perhaps there is a "crowd" in front of Lewis and therefore within fifty feet of the guardsmen. Photograph 51 proves there is not; the cameraman, Howard Ruffner, was standing *behind* Lewis's position, and there simply are no more students, certainly not "ten feet away" as Guardsman Pierce would have us believe.

When Ruffner appeared before the Scranton Commission, he said: "As far as the number of students in this area here [between him and the guardsmen] as General Canterbury mentioned this morning, he said there was a rushing of students and a barrage of rocks. Seeing that I was 120 feet from them, there was only two other students in front of me. I believe one of them was near the sidewalk or just in front of me, along the front of the sidewalk. The one in front of me jumped over the railing as soon as the firing started, and the other one was hit."

Another guardsman, Staff Sergeant Barry Morris of Troop G, told the FBI "the crowd advanced to within 30 feet and was throwing rocks." Sergeant Shafer, also of Troop G, made similar claims to the effect that Joseph Lewis was "advancing on him" and that when Lewis "was 25 to 35 feet away" he shot him. The Justice Department says Lewis "had nothing in his hands," and the FBI says Lewis was standing still, sixty feet away. In contrast to these statements, we have those of Troop G's commander, Captain Srp, SP/4 Robert James of Company A, and Sergeant Richard Love of Company C. The Justice Department reports:

Six Guardsmen, including two sergeants and Captain Srp of Troop G, stated pointedly that the lives of the members of the Guard were not in danger and that it was not a shooting situation . . .

We have some reason to believe that the claim by the National Guard that their lives were endangered by the students was fabricated subsequent to the event . . .

Sergeant Robert James of Company A assumed he'd been given an order to fire, so he fired once in the air. As soon as he saw that some of the men of the 107th (Troop G) were firing into the crowd, he ejected his remaining seven shells so he would not fire any more.

Sergeant Richard Love of Company C fired once in the air, then saw others firing into the crowd; he asserted he "could not believe" that the others were shooting into the crowd, so he lowered his weapon.

The blatant distortions of fact and in some instances obvious falsehoods were inevitable if the guardsmen who deliberately aimed and fired at students were to avoid criminal prosecution. The senior officers too faced possible military discipline if they did not support the testimony of those who started the shooting without orders to do so. When General Del Corso appeared before the Scranton Commission, he was questioned about the Ohio National Guard's guidelines on shooting. His answers provide the key to why the men who violated the guidelines made statements that no photograph or film has substantiated.

Q. Now, with respect to the discharge of weapons, as it is included within the Ohio National Guard training, will you describe what the training and what the regulations are in that area, please?

A. The only time an Ohio National Guardsman is permitted to fire his weapon, unless he is directed to do so by an officer, is for self-defense, to protect the life of himself or another individual.

Q. Now, with respect to self-defense, would you describe what, if any, elaboration is given a guardsman with respect to that rule and that prerequisite to discharge the weapon?

A. Well, in self-defense, if he is being assaulted, and it is apparent that he is going to be seriously injured or possibly killed, this is self-defense, this is close contact.

It has been clearly established that there was no "close contact" just before the shooting. The Justice Department says it has "some reason to believe" that the self-defense excuse was concocted after the shooting, and statements together with photographs confirm the Department's comment. The shooting was not self-defense, nor was it the result of panic. The Justice Department points to the fact that "the Guardsmen were not surrounded. Regardless of the location of the students following them, photographs and television film show that only a very few students were located between the Guard and the Commons. They could easily have continued in the direction in which they had been going."

Three years have passed, and we still do not know why the guardsmen let loose a hail of bullets at students hundreds of feet away. Consequently, we can do no more than what the Justice Department did—"speculate on the possibilities" through an analysis of testimony, official reports, and research findings, using this material in conjunction with the photographs to sift fact from fiction. We have under-taken to do this because Attorney General Mitchell and his successor, Richard Kleindienst, both refused to use the effective tools of dis-covery at their command.

The shooting lasted thirteen seconds. After the final shot was fired, and it is heard distinctly on the tape recording of the gunfire because it comes about one and a half seconds after the cessation of the fusil-lade, one student, Jeffrey Miller, lay dead, three more were dying, one was paralyzed for life, and eight more were bleeding from wounds ranging from serious to minor. Although the official reports of 1970 are in conflict about where, in terms of distances from the guardsmen, some of the victims were at the time they were shot, more recent studies such as Michener's, and my own conversations with survivors, have provided us with the following substantially accurate details:

1. Joseph Lewis, Jr.	71 feet away	Shot while making an obscene gesture. One bullet entered his right lower abdomen and exited from his left buttock. The second bullet caused a through-and-through wound in his lower left leg.
2. John R. Cleary	110 feet away	Shot while standing laterally to the Guard, facing Taylor Hall. The bullet entered his left upper chest, and the main fragments exited from the right upper chest.
3. Thomas Grace	200 feet away	Shot in the back of the left ankle. Fragments exited from the top of his foot.
4. Alan Canfora	225 feet away	Shot in the right wrist, a through-and-through wound.
5. Jeffrey G. Miller	265 feet away	Killed instantly. Shot while facing the Guard. The bullet

entered his mouth and exited at the base of the posterior skull.

6. Dean R. Kahler   300 feet away   Shot in the left posterior side. The bullet traveled from back to front and from above to below, fracturing three vertebrae. He is paralyzed from the waist down and will probably remain a paraplegic.

7. Douglas A. Wrentmore   329 feet away   Shot in the left side of the right knee, causing a compound fracture of the right tibia. The bullet exited on the right side of his knee.

8. Allison B. Krause   343 feet away   Fatally wounded. The autopsy report said immediate cause of death was a gunshot wound with massive hemorrhage, and penetration of the left lower lobe of lung, spleen, stomach, duodenum, liver, and inferior *vena cava*, caused by bullet similar to .30-caliber military ammunition. The bullet had fragmented after penetrating the left upper arm and entering the left lateral chest.

9. James D. Russell   375 feet away   Shot in the right thigh and the right forehead, both injuries minor. Russell was

wounded near the Memorial Gymnasium, an area ninety degrees removed from the location of the other students. A small puncture wound in the right thigh may have been caused by a bullet. The wound to the head may have been caused by birdshot.

10. William K. Schroeder   382 feet away

Fatally wounded. Shot while apparently lying prone on the ground, facing away from the Guard. The bullet entered his left back at the seventh rib, and some fragments exited at the top of his left shoulder.

11. Sandra L. Scheuer   390 feet away

Fatally wounded. Shot through the left front side of her neck. Bullet exited on the right front side, severing her jugular vein. She bled to death as the guardsmen turned on their heels and marched away back down to the ROTC.

12. Robert F. Stamps   495 feet away

Shot in the right buttock. The bullet penetrated four inches. The attending physician expressed the opinion that Stamps was struck by a low-velocity weapon, but

| | | the FBI's lab analysis shows the bullet came from a military weapon. |
| 13. Donald S. MacKenzie | 730 feet away | Shot while running in the opposite direction from the Guard. The bullet entered the left rear of his neck, struck his jawbone, and exited through his cheek. |

The descriptions of each wound, with the exception of the autopsy report on Allison, were taken from the Justice Department's summary of the FBI report. They tell, clinically, the full horror of what happened at Kent State on May 4, and the staggering distances make the Guard's claim of self-defense not only ridiculous but contemptible. Not one of the guardsmen who aimed and fired at the students—not the ones who have admitted doing so or the ones who have not—could successfully have argued self-defense as a civilian before a district attorney. But Americans have evidently come to regard the uniform as sacrosanct. If soldiers say they fired in self-defense, then they did, since military men never lie.

The next sequence of photographs, 55 to 57, shows what was happening at the entrance to the parking lot, in the southern end of the lot, and at the northern end of the adjacent football practice field. Everyone in these photographs is over two hundred feet away from the guardsmen and either running away or lying flat on the ground. William Schroeder was lying prone just like the students in photo 57 when a bullet slammed into his back. The most damning evidence against the Guard is the fact that their shooting was directed into this area, with the result that eleven of the thirteen students shot were two hundred feet or more from the Pagoda. *If the guardsmen's claim that a crowd was charging them to within ten, fifteen, twenty, and thirty feet was true, then obviously most of the casualties would have been less than two hundred feet away. Why were they shooting at students two hundred, three hundred, and four hundred feet away from them, distances that removed any danger whatever to the soldiers?*

The wildness of the Guard's claims is apparent when one looks at the photographs. Here's Michener's account: "One official who was responsible for studying all aspects of the situation says flatly, 'If they hadn't fired, they would have been killed.' General Canterbury testifies that they were in danger of their lives. The official statement of the

55

Guardsmen issued after the firing agrees that the men were in mortal danger from which they could extricate themselves only with gunfire, and numerous witnesses, some of whom appear not to have been at the scene, testify to hordes of students about to overrun the Guardsmen." These statements are without evidence to substantiate them. Were it not for the bloody toll, they would be comical. Even the Justice Department has pointedly discredited them and has suggested that they were "fabricated" after the shooting.

In photograph 51 it appears that General Canterbury and several members of Company A have just reacted to the sound of shots. In photo 52 Canterbury can be seen approaching the front line of guardsmen. He testified that he immediately ordered the men to cease fire. No one has disputed this testimony. In photograph 58 Canterbury has finally reached the line and appears to be physically trying to stop the last few men of Troop G who are still shooting. The big guardsman in the center of the line, also seen in photograph 52 aiming in the direction of the parking lot, is now aiming much closer toward the railing in the direction of where Joseph Lewis, Jr., was standing when he was shot. It is this guardsman that Canterbury appears to be trying to restrain from further shooting, although there are a few more with rifles in aiming position.

The man identified by the Akron *Beacon Journal* as Sergeant Pryor has ceased whatever it was he was doing in photographs 44 and 45 and, according to the Scranton Commission, "appears to be ejecting shells from his weapon." One cannot help but wonder why, in view of the sergeant's comments, which range from a denial that he was on the hill, through a concession that it might be he, to a claim that he was loading his .45 rather than firing it, and culminate in the flat statement that at all times on May 4, 1970, his .45 contained an empty magazine. It is quite impossible to reconcile this statement with the man's stance and action in photo 52—but there it is: he is aiming an empty gun while guardsmen all around and behind him are shooting away at students in the parking lot.

If there is a panoramic photograph that totally discredits the Ohio National Guard's claim that the men fired because their lives were in mortal danger from a "charging mob," it is Beverly K. Knowles's dramatic picture taken from Prentice Hall, photo 60. In this shot we can see the guardsmen at the Pagoda and the four students they killed. The Knowles photograph is invaluable and presumably played no small part in the Justice Department's conclusions regarding the Guard's claims of self-defense. Here those distances of 265, 343, 382, and 390 feet become visually discernible. Also, we see just how large the parking-lot crowd really was at the time of the shooting.

Photographs 61 through 64 record the final act on the part of the Ohio National Guard: regrouping, turning on their heels, and march-

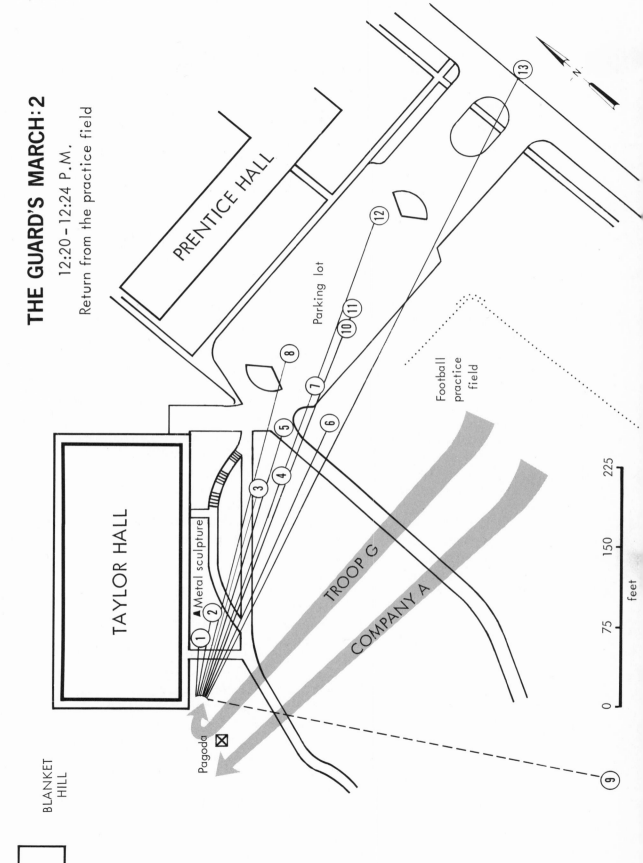

THE GUARD'S MARCH: 2

12:20 – 12:24 P.M.
Return from the practice field

THE COMMONS

BLANKET HILL

TAYLOR HALL

PRENTICE HALL

▲Metal sculpture

Parking lot

Pagoda

Football
practice
field

TROOP G

COMPANY A

0   75   150   225

feet

N

ing back down the Commons to the point they had started out from just thirty minutes earlier.

The next series of photographs reveals a little of the havoc the guardsmen left behind when they departed from the Pagoda. In fact, professional medical aid did not arrive for almost fifteen minutes. The ambulances were behind the Guard's rope line at the foot of the Commons until 12:45. Eszterhas and Roberts describe the incident leading to the release of the ambulances: "Michael Stein, watching from Blanket Hill, saw a coed run toward the guardsmen on the Commons with her hands over her head to make sure she wouldn't be shot. She was Pam Holland, a sophomore. An ambulance stood next to the guardsmen. 'As I ran down,' Pam said, 'I was screaming obscenities. I wasn't in any way to be talked to.' She screamed, 'People are dying, get the ambulances up there!' One of the guardsmen came up to her, shoved her, and said, 'Where's your identification?' She kept screaming, 'Get a doctor!' They finally sent the ambulance up."

While some of the guardsmen were in a daze as to what had happened and some were close to tears, there were a few who felt quite differently. Major John Simons, chaplain of the 107th Armored (Troop G), told Eszterhas and Roberts that the first guardsman he spoke to on their arrival back at ROTC said, "I fired right down the gully." Simons noted that "there was hate on the guy's face" and he thought, "You just can't get away from it. This guy placed one exactly where he wanted to." While most of the guardsmen wondered what had happened, the students were too stunned to believe what they had witnessed. As they gathered around the victims and tried to help, the wail of sirens signaled the arrival of ambulances—not enough, however, for the number in need of medical attention. Only one student, Jeffrey Miller, was beyond help. He had died instantly. When the last of the dead and wounded had been removed, a sanitation truck drove into the parking lot to hose away the blood.

So we are left with a host of unanswered questions. Just exactly what is the left-handed guardsman with the .45 doing in photographs 51 and 52? Whom do the four spent .45 cartridges belong to? Who are the two or more guardsmen the Justice Department says lied to federal agents? How much longer are we expected to accept the ridiculous claim by the five men of Troop G that they fired a total of only "eight shots into the crowd or at a specific student?" These are the only guardsmen who have admitted shooting at someone, which means that with eight bullets they inflicted thirteen wounds (not including Russell's birdshot injuries) and, according to the FBI, put more than thirty holes into cars parked in the parking lot. Photographs 71 and 72 show one of the holes and two smashed windows. An inquiry seeking answers to these questions is clearly called for. Not because such an inquiry would restore life to the dead or mobility to

58

Dean Kahler's legs, but because we live by laws that no guardsman is above and no student below. President Nixon said in his December 10, 1970, letter to William Scranton: "A human life—the life of a student, soldier, or police officer—is a precious thing, and the taking of a life can be justified only as a necessary last resort."

Those guardsmen who aimed and fired into the crowd or at specific students have had every excuse for their action rejected or discredited by the Department of Justice. The great weight of available evidence indicates that they acted without the law; that they violated their victims' Constitutional rights; that they violated the Ohio Revised Code, which holds members of the Guard, like all other citizens, responsible for the killing or wounding of individuals except where such action is accidental, in self-defense, or "necessary and proper to suppress a riot or disperse or apprehend rioters." The force used has already been officially condemned as unnecessary and improper. Eight months later, Attorney General John Mitchell found the shooting and its consequences not only "unnecessary" but "inexcusable." Both the Justice Department and the Scranton Commission have found that there was no riot at the time the Guard fired tear gas at the students. And no court of law has yet made a determination regarding the authority on which General Canterbury violated the constitutional right of Kent State's 20,000 student body to assemble peacefully on the Commons. Finally, there is no question that the Guard violated Section 7-4, paragraph d of the Army field manual regulations pertaining to control of civil disturbances: "The use of deadly force (i.e., live ammunition or any other type of physical force likely to cause death or serious bodily harm) in effect invokes the power of summary execution and can therefore be justified only by extreme necessity. Accordingly, its use is not authorized for the purpose of preventing activities which do not pose a significant risk of death or serious bodily harm (for example, curfew violations or looting)."

One other admonition against the use of lethal force contained in the Army field manual bears quoting here because it refers to the kind of shooting that took place at Kent State: "(5) Full Firepower—The most severe measure of force that can be applied by troops is that of available unit firepower with the intent of producing extensive casualties. This extreme measure would be used as a last resort only after all other measures have failed or obviously would be impractical, and the consequence of failure to completely subdue the riot would be imminent overthrow of the government, continued mass casualties, or similar grievous conditions." The paragraph concludes with the heartening sentence that full firepower has "never been used by Federal troops." Does this indicate, then, that when National Guardsmen are federalized, there is superior discipline and command control, compared to the more numerous occasions when they are activated by a state? Yet, even the Ohio National Guard had not resorted to lethal force during Del Corso's tenure as its adjutant general. For some reason, Kent State was different from all other confrontations, even ones in which snipers opened fire. Why was Kent State different? Until we get the extensive and impartial investigation the four deaths demand, the limited evidence now available suggests only one answer: it was different because a few guardsmen decided among themselves to "get the bastards" that had given them so much trouble since noon, and upon a set signal they turned in unison and opened fire on targets two hundred feet and more away from them. In so doing, they caused panic and confusion to sweep through the rest of the Guard, triggering another twenty or more men to fire, some into the air, some into the ground, and at least one into the crowd. Only a thorough investigation by the Justice Department or by a joint committee of the House and Senate Judiciary Committees can dispel the impression, conveyed by photographs, the testimony, and official reports, that this is what happened. If, as the Ohio National Guard insists, this impression is totally erroneous and contrary to the facts, why has the Ohio National Guard obstructed every effort to root out the truth, instead of calling for an investigation, if only to settle the issue once and for all?

1 Aerial view of the Kent State campus, Taylor Hall in the center

Akron-Beacon Journal, Ted Walls

2 The noon rally. Arrow points to a figure identified as Terry Norman, a photographer alleged to have been working for the FBI or the campus police

3 The line of the National Guard in front of the ruins of the ROTC building

4 Gen. Canterbury, in civilian clothes, with the guardsmen facing the students gathered for the noon rally

5 Students gathered for the noon rally, some taunting the guardsmen

Akron-Beacon Journal, Don Roese

6 Kent State policeman Harold Rice, in the jeep, reads the Riot Act to the peaceful crowd assembled for the noon rally. In the background is Taylor Hall and to the far right is Blanket Hill

Kent State University News Service

7 Guardsmen assemble to carry out Gen. Canterbury's order to disperse the noon rally

Kent State University News Service

Kent State University News Service

8 Behind a barrage of tear gas, 113 officers and men of the Ohio National Guard start out on their mission to disperse the noon rally. Students in the background were ignored by the Guard, who considered them spectators rather than demonstrators. This contributed to the "circus" atmosphere described by several witnesses

9 Front view of guardsmen advancing up the slope of the Commons toward the students. Gen. Canterbury is in the center in civilian clothes

10 Rear view of guardsmen advancing on the students. The news-media cameraman on the left did not stay with the Guard but remained on the Commons and was there when the troops came back down this same slope after the shooting

11 The center of the National Guard line draws closer to Taylor Hall. Streamer of tear gas is from a canister thrown back at the Guard. News cameraman is still with the advancing guardsmen but will shortly stop and stay behind. Man standing on the roof of Taylor Hall is a photographer with tripod camera

12 The bulk of the students begin to swarm up Blanket Hill at the western end of Taylor Hall. A few stand their ground temporarily. Most, however, have their backs to the guardsmen

Kent State University News Service

13 Troop G, on the left, are now close to their initial objective:
clearing the Commons by marching to the western end of Taylor Hall

14 Gen. Canterbury's mission to disperse the noon rally has been accomplished. The Commons has been cleared of both demonstrators and spectators

15 View, from Johnson Hall, of guardsmen's ascent of Blanket Hill. A few students are lingering at the crest

Akron-Beacon Journal, Chuck Ayres

16 Members of Troop G climbing Blanket Hill toward the Pagoda. Allison Krause is just to the right of the Pagoda shouting at the approaching guardsmen

17 Students fleeing the Commons as the guardsmen approach the west side of Taylor Hall

Akron-Beacon Journal

18 Near the northeast corner of Taylor Hall: the first known face-to-face clash between a civilian and a guardsman

Kent State University News Service

20 The first time guardsmen aim their weapons at students

21 Guardsmen on football field. Troop G to extreme left, facing the parking lot some one hundred feet away. Tri-Towers in background. Young men in foreground are at the foot of the Taylor Hall slope

Akron-Beacon Journal

William A. Ling

22 Students in Prentice Hall parking lot throw rocks at the Guard

William A. Ling

23 A guardsman throws a rock back at the students

Akron-Beacon Journal

24 At the far end of the Prentice Hall parking lot, about five students can be seen throwing objects or running toward the fence. The distance to the guardsmen on the football field, at right, speaks for itself

Beverly K. Knowles

25 The much larger crowd is located on the Taylor Hall slope, not in the parking lot. Yet the National Guard later claimed the students seen here in the lot, along with those out of sight to the left, posed a dire threat to the men. Another photo by Beverly K. Knowles (26) spans the area from beyond the car on the left all the way to the eastern exits of the parking lot and the long chain fence that stopped the Guard's march

Beverly K. Knowles

26 Michener called this photograph "remarkable" because it confirmed what photos 24 and 25 might have missed (the "hordes," or absence thereof) because they were taken from blind angles. Michener, in examining this picture, says: "To the south, there are no students for at least two hundred yards; much of the field is visible and completely empty. To the east not one student can be seen behind the fence. And where the mob was supposed to have been there was only empty space for nearly forty yards, then the high steel fence of the baseball diamond, then the parking lot. On or near it could be counted about a score of students, five of them, with books under their arms, walking away from the Guard." Yet at this moment Troop G are kneeling and aiming their M-1 rifles in the direction of this so-called mob

27 Another view of students in the parking lot

John P. Filo; © 1970 Valley Daily News, Tarentum, Pa.

28 Guardsmen kneel and aim at the students in the parking lot

29 Student in front of Taylor Hall throws a tear-gas canister back at the guardsmen on the practice field

30 A tear-gas canister, thrown back by a student, lands on the football practice field behind the kneeling men of Troop G, who are aiming their rifles at students in the parking lot some 150 feet away

Mike Glaser

31 A guardsman picks up the tear-gas canister and throws it back toward the students on the slope of Taylor Hall. Bottom center is the tollgate entrance to the Prentice Hall parking lot

Mike Glaser

32 View from the slope in front of Taylor Hall, with the parking lot to extreme right. Guardsmen are aiming in that direction

Akron-Beacon Journal

John P. Filo; © 1970 Valley Daily News, Tarentum, Pa.

33 This photograph was taken almost at the identical moment as the preceding photo, only the cameraman here is near the western end of the parking lot. Tear gas is presumably from the canister seen in photos 30 and 31

34 Students at eastern end of the parking lot harass the guardsmen in the practice field

35 Guardsman throws back tear-gas canister

36 A student taunts the Guard with a black flag

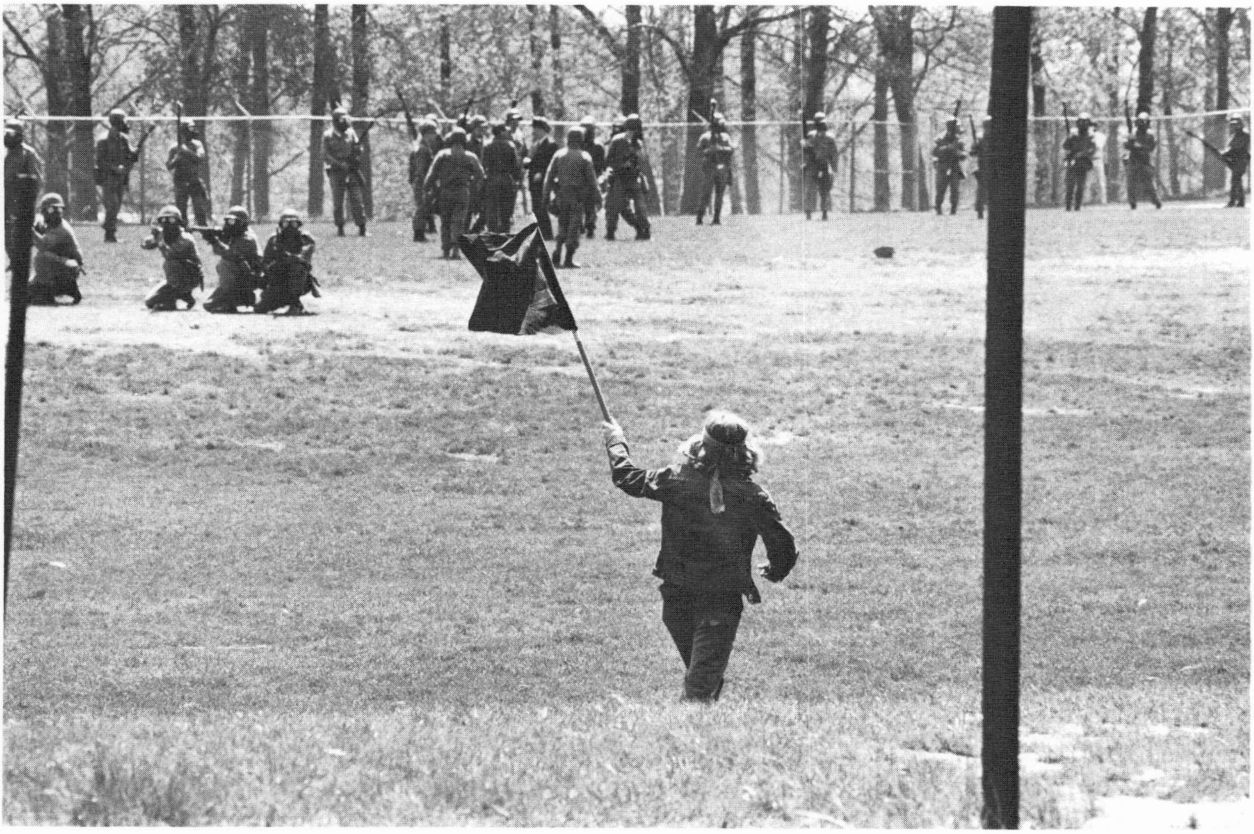

37 The Guard starts to leave the practice field. Troop G is on the left

Kent State University News Service

38

John P. Filo; © 1970 Valley Daily News, Tarentum, Pa.

39

40

John P. Filo; © 1970 Valley Daily News, Tarentum, Pa.

41 The Guard starts to climb the hill toward the Pagoda

John P. Filo; © 1970 Valley Daily News, Tarentum, Pa.

43 Some of the guardsmen turn to look back at the parking lot as they continue up the hill

John P. Filo; © 1970 Valley Daily News, Tarentum, Pa.

45 Another view of the climb, with Troop G on the left

Akron-Beacon Journal

46 A view of the metal sculpture (on the right), with few students
in evidence

47 Company A approaching the crest of the hill, accompanied by two civilians; the one on the right appears to be Terry Norman

48 A view from the far end of the parking lot, as guardsmen approach the Pagoda. In less than a minute, some of them will turn and fire in the direction of the camera

49 Seconds away from the shooting, the guardsmen reach the Pagoda

50 Some of the guardsmen have turned and are about to fire

51 Another view of the same moment, taken from the terrace of Taylor Hall

52 Here the guardsmen are shooting. Gen. Canterbury moves forward from extreme right of picture

John A. Darnell, Jr.

53 The students react by fleeing the terrace area. Joseph Lewis is in the center of the photo on the other side of the railing, taunting the guardsmen with upraised finger

Akron-Beacon Journal

54 A picture taken the next day, looking at the Prentice Hall parking lot from the Pagoda. Almost all the shots were aimed between the metal sculpture on the left and the two pine trees on the right

55 Students running for cover 250 feet from the guardsmen at the Pagoda (behind cameraman). Further away is where Allison Krause, Sandy Scheuer, and Bill Schroeder fell, and Jeff Miller was hit several yards to the right in the roadway

56 Another view of students running for cover in the parking lot

57 Northern end of the football practice field. The worn patch of grass, upper left, is where Troop G was positioned during the Guard's stay before their return march to the Commons. The girl lying prone, near the patch, is a good 450 feet from the guardsmen

Kent State University News Service

John A. Darnell, Jr.

58 Gen. Canterbury, wearing a gas mask atop his head, has moved just behind the front rank of shooters as he orders them to cease fire. At far left, the guardsman with the pistol in his left hand appears to be ejecting shells from his weapon

John A. Darnell, Jr.

59 The shooting has stopped. Maj. Jones, in the foreground, seems to be restraining his men from further firing

Beverly K. Knowles

60 The four students killed are indicated as follows: (1) William Schroeder, (2) Sandra Scheuer, (3) Jeffrey Miller, (4) Allison Krause. The Pagoda and guardsmen can be seen in the upper right corner

61 In the foreground lies Joseph Lewis, Jr., shot twice

Kent State University News Service

62 Kneeling students, at right, surround John Cleary, shot while standing facing Taylor Hall 110 feet away from the guardsmen

63 As the guardsmen turn on their heels and depart, students try to help Joseph Lewis, Jr., who has been gravely wounded

Kent State University News Service

64 The Guard marches back to its lines, leaving behind one dead, three dying, and nine wounded

65 Jeffrey Miller lies dead, 265 feet from the guardsman who killed him

John P. Filo; © 1970 Valley Daily News, Tarentum, Pa.

66 The Guard now gone, the students converge on the Taylor Hall terrace

67 The scene in the parking lot just after the shooting

Akron-Beacon Journal

68 Students looking after John Cleary, awaiting medical aid

69 Allison Krause being carried on a stretcher to an ambulance

70 Jeffrey Miller

71 One of the few dozen bullet holes in automobiles in the Prentice Hall parking lot

72 The shattered windows of a car in the parking lot

73 Gen. Canterbury, on the right, warning faculty and student representatives that students who have reassembled on the Commons must disperse within fifteen minutes or he will order the Guard out again

74 Terry Norman, the freelance photographer, inside the Guard line

three
Reaction and Inaction

When dissent turns to violence, it invites tragedy.

President Nixon
May 5, 1970

The grief, dismay, anger, and in some quarters satisfaction over the killings at Kent State were still intense when, just ten days later, two more students were shot and killed on a college campus. Phillip Gibbs, a married, twenty-year-old junior and the father of an eighteen-month-old child, was standing near the west wing doorway of Alexander Hall at Jackson State College in Mississippi when a twenty-eight-second barrage of police gunfire cut him down. James Earl Green, an eighteen-year-old high-school student, was standing in front of Roberts Hall at the time the firing started. As he ran for cover, a buckshot pellet struck him in the side and ripped through his liver, left lung, and heart. Twelve others were wounded, six of them women, all but one of whom were inside Alexander Hall, which, the Scranton Commission reported, was hit by "nearly 400 bullets or pieces of buckshot."

The commission's investigation of the shootings at Jackson State revealed that a "majority" of the policemen and Mississippi Highway Patrolmen fired their weapons at the west wing of Alexander Hall, using "buckshot, rifle slugs, a submachine gun, carbines with military ammunition, and two 30.06 rifles loaded with armor-piercing bullets." The law-enforcement officers, or, as the Scranton Commission described them at one point in its report, the peace officers, also had on hand the Mississippi National Guard and an armored vehicle known as "Thompson's tank" after former Jackson Mayor Thompson, who had ordered the purchase of the anti-riot vehicle. The commission, however, failed to find any evidence to support the by-now predictable police claim that they were fired at by snipers.

The shooting at Jackson State was preceded by disturbances on May 13 that culminated on the fourteenth with a fire: the burning of a dump truck. Around 10:15 in the evening of the fourteenth, reports were coming to the Jackson police department to the effect that the situation on campus was deteriorating. The Scranton Commission confirmed that a policeman then issued a radio order: "Call that security guard out there at Jackson State and see if they can't scatter them niggers." Less than two hours later, the demonstrators were scattered by more than 150 rounds of buckshot, rifle slugs, and bullets, with one patrolman firing four rounds and then reloading and firing off four more rounds and then reloading yet again and firing. He told the commission "he did not know how many times he reloaded and emptied his gun."

The incident at Jackson State, coming so soon after Kent State, added momentum to the reaction of students, which resulted in the only national student strike in the country's history. But if, for a great many campus moderates, the shootings were inexcusable, a majority of their parents felt that the resort to lethal force was long overdue. Unable, or unwilling, to administer the spankings they believed their sons and daughters deserved, many parents were only too eager to register approval of the killings, and in so doing implied that M-1 bullets and buckshot are an acceptable substitution for a parental whack on the bottom. As James Michener discovered, much to his dismay, a "depressing number" of the four hundred Kent State students interviewed by the researchers for his book "had been told by their parents that it might have been a good thing if they had been shot." Unfortunately, Michener's dismay did not prevent him from saying it was "only charitable to point out that many of the women [mothers] spoke in temporary anger, expressing themselves more harshly than intended." Anger at what? At the students for getting killed?

This reaction among Kent State parents was by no means untypical. In the weeks that followed the shootings, many Americans formulated opinions about what had happened, based on distorted accounts in the newspapers. Even some editorial comment implied approval of the shootings, before many of the facts were known. The news media generally accepted President Nixon's statement that "when dissent turns to violence, it invites tragedy," an observation which the vice president of the Union of American Hebrew Congregations, Rabbi Alexander M. Schindler, found particularly offensive. Speaking in Cleveland on May 9, 1970, Rabbi Schindler condemned the "tragic reaction of those in authority" and charged that "Nixon perversely twists the meaning of this disaster to judge the victims guilty and to hold the killers blameless." Yet the President's disregard for the lives taken at Kent State struck a receptive chord in the electorate.

Few people bothered to find out what had turned dissent into violence, nor did the public seem disturbed when the Scranton Commission issued its report almost five months later, finding that the noon rally had been a "peaceful assembly" and that "only when the Guard attempted to disperse the rally did some students react violently." This official confirmation that the rights of the students had been violated by the Ohio National Guard came too late, because the molders of public opinion had successfully established a picture of May 4 in the minds of the people which no official reports were going to dispel. Syndicated columnist Victor Riesel's article of May 9, 1970, was typical of the misinformation and innuendo the public was being fed. It had been proved, he claimed, that the SDS Weatherman faction had brought about the confrontation with the National Guard. "Intelligence sources," he said, "have been reporting Kent State U. as the target for years." Note, he said, SDS demands at Kent State such as "End project Themis Grant to the Liquid Crystals Institute." SDS, he failed to mention, had been banned from Kent State for over a year. "There are but two such institutes in our land," he went on. One was at Kent State, and its purpose was to develop "liquid crystal detectors," of "vital strategic use" to American troops in Vietnam. These detectors supposedly helped locate hidden Vietcong and North Vietnamese troops, being "extremely sensitive to heat" generated by campfires and by the human body. Riesel's article appeared in May, but the Justice Department was not heard from until many months later when in its summary of the FBI investigation it stated that Kent State was not engaged in the development of liquid crystal detectors and "rumors" to the contrary were quite erroneous.

Riesel did not limit himself to the institute story. He went so far as to state that the "toughest band of nihilists this land has known" had chosen Kent State as the object of their revolutionary rhetoric; therefore, the SDS, not the Ohio National Guard, was responsible for the blood "now rotting the earth of Kent's lovely campus." He tied this conclusion to the fact that Bernardine Dohrn had visited the campus in April 1969 and had addressed the students. Indeed, there had been disturbances, and the Kent State chapter of SDS, which had a membership of less than one half of one percent of the university's enrollment, was closed and the organization ejected from the campus. The Justice Department dismissed any connection between the SDS and the disturbances of May 1–4, 1970. Even the release from prison of four campus SDS leaders on the eve of the May 4 confrontation was irrelevant, as found by the Justice Department. They had been arrested during the 1969 melee and had been tried and convicted, and their release provided fuel for those engaged in spreading rumors about SDS involvement in the demonstrations that led to the shooting. "Although there has been speculation in local law-enforcement circles," the Justice Department says, "that [the four] participated or even planned the confrontations occurring May 1–4, 1970, there is no evidence to substantiate this. Similarly, although Jerry Rubin made a speech at Kent State on April 10, 1970, no connection has been made between that speech and the May 1–4 weekend. To our knowledge, from April 1969 until May 1, 1970, Kent State University experienced no problems with student unrest." If any evidence had existed, as Riesel claimed it did, it is inconceivable that the FBI under the direction of J. Edgar Hoover and the Justice Department under the aegis of Attorney General John Mitchell would not have uncovered it.

In less than a week, the events at Kent State had been so distorted that it became impossible even for those of a moderate conservative persuasion to see beyond the burning ROTC building and the rock throwing. Blinded by false images, more than sixty percent of the American public condoned the shooting, according to a *Newsweek* poll. This general approval of the guardsmen's actions must have given the Administration a clear indication of the course it should take, even if the FBI found no evidence to substantiate the Guard's claim of self-defense. When the FBI finally turned over its 8,000-page report to the Civil Rights Division of the Justice Department, government lawyers were hard put to find any satisfactory explanation, let alone justification, for the shooting. There was a sharp division of opinion, then, within the Department, on the question of a grand jury. Robert Murphy, deputy chief of the Criminal Section of the Civil Rights Division, felt the circumstances warranted federal intervention, and so did his colleague, Robert Hocutt, who had participated in the Justice Department's prosecution of nine South Carolina highway patrolmen for the killing of three students on the campus of South Carolina State College at Orangeburg in 1968. Mr. Hocutt resigned from the Justice Department before Attorney General Mitchell publicly announced the Administration's decision to do nothing in the Kent State case, a decision disclosed after sixteen months of evasion and procrastination.

The Scranton Commission

On June 13, 1970, President Nixon sought to allay student unrest and delay any federal action by announcing the convening of a commission to examine campus disturbances in general and the killings at Kent State and Jackson State in particular. He appointed former Republican governor of Pennsylvania William Scranton as chairman and empowered him to subpoena witnesses. This important tool was rendered virtually useless, however, by the imposition of a time limit on the investigation: the commission must submit their report to Nixon no later than October 1, so he might demonstrate to the millions of students returning to their campuses the alacrity with which he had dealt with the problems troubling young citizens. The deadline provided Ohio National Guardsmen with the perfect loophole for evading the subpoenas served on them by the commission. In fact, no guardsman actually involved in the shooting appeared before the Scranton Commission, and the veil of secrecy which had enveloped these men since May 4 was effectively preserved.

The first intimation that President Nixon planned to convene a commission came on May 25, when Presidential news aide Herbert Klein disclosed that "a high-level commission to get to the bottom of the facts" would soon be appointed. On the same day, Joe Eszterhas wrote in his article "Ohio Honors Its Dead," "another White House press aide, Gerald Warren, 'clarified' Klein and said the purpose of the commission 'wouldn't necessarily be to get to the bottom of the facts of the shooting,' but that it would be a 'broad study.' " In other words, the Nixon Administration was less interested in getting at the truth than it was in producing a document that had the appearance of thoroughness.

The selection of the commission members could hardly be faulted. In fact, a few felt that it was going to be impossible for them to work together as a team, so well balanced were they. The military viewpoint was represented by Benjamin O. Davis, a retired Air Force general, and the student position by Joseph Rhodes, Jr., a junior fellow at Harvard. Law enforcement and its problems in a civil disturbance were represented by James F. Ahern, the chief of the New Haven, Connecticut, police department. Even a member of the press was chosen to be one of the nine—the editor-in-chief of the *Christian Science Monitor,* Erwin D. Canham. Legal aspects of the cases on both campuses would be assessed by Bayless Manning, dean of the Stanford University School of Law, and Revius O. Ortique, Jr., a practicing attorney in New Orleans. James E. Cheek, president of Howard University, joined Martha Derthick, associate professor at Boston College, as spokesmen for the academic community. With William Scranton as chairman, there was every reason to believe these nine citizens would be fair and do their best under the deadline imposed by the President.

The large staff that a Presidential commission needs to accomplish its task was under the direction of Wm. Matthew Byrne, Jr., now a federal judge in California, and it is to his credit that the men and women who worked so diligently in research, writing, and field operations were able to produce the 537-page report in just three months.

The Scranton Commission held its first meeting on June 25, 1970, and conducted thirteen days of public hearings in Washington, D.C., Los Angeles, Jackson, and Kent. The Washington session was designed to provide the commission with a cross section of opinion regarding campus unrest. Among the twenty-six witnesses called to testify were Senator Edward M. Kennedy, Charles F. Palmer, president of the National Student Association, Senator Hugh Scott, and Major General Winston P. Wilson, chief of the National Guard Bureau. It was during General Wilson's appearance before the commission that a sharp exchange took place when the general displayed a selection of rocks and hardware allegedly similar to what had been thrown at guardsmen on the Kent State campus. A member of the commission wondered if the material before him were equal in destructive power to an M-1 rifle.

The commission went to Jackson State College in August and held public hearings from August 11 to 13, during which time twenty-four persons testified, among them four members of the Jackson police department, two members of the Mississippi Highway Safety Patrol, and Walter Johnson, adjutant general of the Mississippi National Guard. Six days later the commission moved to Kent, Ohio, where it took testimony from an equal number of witnesses. Ten of the twenty-four witnesses were students. But none of the guardsmen who fired their weapons testified. In fact, only one member of the Ohio National Guard who was present on the campus on May 4 appeared before the commission: Brigadier General Robert Canterbury, deputy adjutant general. This in spite of the fact that the joint Congressional resolution granting various powers to the commission specifically denied any witness duly subpoenaed by the commission the right to "refuse to comply with the order on the basis of his privilege against self-incrimination." The resolution protected the witnesses by declaring that "no testimony or other information compelled under the order (or any information directly or indirectly derived from such testimony or other information) may be used against the witness in any criminal case, except a prosecution for perjury, giving a false statement, or otherwise failing to comply with the order."

Captain Srp, however, along with Lieutenant Alexander Stevenson, also of Troop G, filed suit in federal court in Cleveland to have the subpoenas vacated on the grounds that their appearance before the commission might prejudice their rights in the forthcoming Ohio grand-jury investigation. Had the Scranton Commission possessed a stiffer backbone, it could justifiably have shifted the onus for any delay in completing their work onto the shoulders of Ohio National Guard officers who were prepared to use every legal means available to avoid the witness stand. But, though the commission had Congressional authority to enforce the subpoenas, they withdrew them.

General Canterbury testified that the situation on the hill had been "critical" and, just before the shooting, was so dangerous that "many members of this commission would have fired." He spoke about a mob of students throwing "hundreds" of rocks at his men. The general asserted that Kent State president Robert White was the man responsible for ordering the peaceful noon rally dispersed by force of arms, a statement that White flatly denied. Both men had testified under oath. The commission did not resolve the contradiction.

General Sylvester Del Corso, adjutant general of the Ohio National

Guard, was in Columbus on the day of the shooting, but some of his testimony was illuminating. During his appearance before the commission, there was this exchange between him and commission member Erwin Canham:

Q. Did I accurately understand when you said that you could envisage no commander giving an order to fire into a crowd?
A. That is right.
Q. Then is it your suggestion that the commander might not assess the situation as being endangering to the lives of his forces? That is to say, why doesn't he think the same way as the individual troops?
A. Well, I am certain he does assess this all of the time. Commanders are doing this all of the time they are in command, continuously assessing the situation or attempting to do what is the best procedure to maintain peace and order.
Q. And you are suggesting that the commander under these circumstances did not assess it as requiring fire?
A. No. I won't say that.

Canterbury's position in the photographs, however, is illuminating. Like most of his men, he apparently had his back to the students when the first shot rang out. Could the situation have been as "critical" as he would have us believe? The experience of the Ohio National Guard had been such that none of the officers had reason to expect the men to open fire, as Del Corso indicated when he told the commission:

As a matter of fact, in all the commitments that our troops have been committed, which have been more than any other community in the United States Army, we have never injured an individual until the Kent State incident.

Yet, in every incident, we have had our troops injured, we have been fired at in many of them, and certainly we have taken verbal insults.

The Scranton Commission concluded its hearings at Kent State on August 21 without summoning Ohio's Governor James A. Rhodes, the man responsible for sending the National Guard to Kent.

On September 26, 1970, William W. Scranton submitted the commission's report to President Nixon. Public release of the special report on Kent State was delayed until 6 P.M. Sunday, October 4. As for the report on campus unrest in general, it had scarcely been analyzed by the nation's press before Vice President Agnew condemned it as "pablum for permissiveness." Other conservative Republicans responded to the cue, and in short order the Scranton Commission became the object of political barbs. The President remained silent until December, though in the conclusion to their general report, the commission said "the most important aspect of the overall effort to prevent further campus disorder—indeed, the most important of all the Commission's recommendations—rests with the President. As the leader of all Americans, only the President can offer the compassionate, reconciling moral leadership that can bring the country together again. Only the President has the platform and prestige to urge all Americans, at once, to step back from the battle lines into which they are forming. Only the President, by example and by instruction, can effectively calm the rhetoric of both public officials and protestors whose words in the past have too often helped further divide the country, rather than unite it."

The commission had failed to come up with any explanation for the shooting at Kent State and, in the belief that the Justice Department would convene a federal grand jury, had avoided touching on any possible criminal aspects of the Ohio National Guard's conduct. In the conclusion to their special report on Kent State, the commission stated that, although the killings constituted a national tragedy, it was not a unique tragedy: "Only the magnitude of the student disorder and the extent of student deaths and injuries set it apart from similar occurrences on numerous other American campuses during the past few years." The throwing of rocks, the waving of black flags, and the verbal abuse on the part of students are described by the commission as "violent and criminal" and "dangerous, reckless, and irresponsible." The aiming and firing of M-1 rifles and .45 pistols into a crowd of demonstrators, observers, and passers-by is described as "unnecessary, unwarranted and inexcusable." In rendering this sharp definition between the criminal and dangerous actions of the students and the unnecessary actions of the Ohio National Guard, the commission overlooked its own findings that the May 4 rally "began as a peaceful assembly on the Commons—the traditional site of student assemblies"; that "the decision to disperse the noon rally was a serious error"; and that "only when the Guard attempted to disperse the rally did some students react violently."

The report condemned as unjustified the "general issuance of loaded weapons to law-enforcement officers engaged in controlling disorders," except "in the case of armed resistance that trained snipers are unable to handle." This "was not the case at Kent State" the commission noted. "Yet each guardsman carried a loaded M-1 rifle." The confrontation, it was conceded, was "engendered in part by their [the guardsmen's] own activities"; even "if the guardsmen faced danger, it was not a danger that called for lethal force."

On December 10, 1970, President Nixon responded to the commission's report with an eleven-page letter to Governor Scranton. In the first paragraph the President intimated his displeasure with the commission's remarks about leadership and the Presidency. He noted that although he had been about to leave for Europe at the time the report was submitted, he had ordered it released to the public because "it is as much or more addressed to students, professors and academic administrators, and to the public generally, as to the Federal Government."

On the question of Presidential responsibility, Nixon said that "moral authority in a great and diverse nation such as ours does not reside in the Presidency alone. There are thousands upon thousands of individuals—clergy, teachers, public officials, scholars, writers—to whom segments of the nation look for moral, intellectual and political leadership." The families of the dead and wounded at Kent State would, indeed, have to look elsewhere for the moral leadership their President had failed to provide them.

Perhaps the best critique of the Scranton Commission and its report came from the pen of I. F. Stone in the October 19, 1970, issue of his *Bi-Weekly:*

> The danger in the Jackson State and Kent State reports by the President's Commission on Campus Unrest lies in their very quality. If they had white-washed the killings, the findings would be angrily dismissed by blacks and students as more-of-the-same, but the hope would remain that a better investigation by better men might have produced better results. The destructive potential of the reports comes from the fact that they have honestly and thoroughly shown that the killings were unjustified and unnecessary. The established order mustered its best and they fulfilled their moral and political obligation. And yet there is not the slightest chance that anything will be done about it . . .
>
> The Commission can be criticised on two points. Its main business was to investigate the killings at Jackson State and Kent State but it chose to issue its findings on these in two separate reports released several days after its main report. These two were released separately and without specially televised briefings. Governor Scranton and his colleagues could have put on the nation's television screens their conclusion that the killings on both campuses were unjustified and unnecessary. They chose instead to televise the safe and even-handed generalities of their main recommendations, and left town before the other reports were issued. Apparently all the advance criticism orchestrated by the White House and Agnew had made them afraid of becoming too controversial. The other criticism is that these two reports do not put the spotlight on those responsible for the killings . . .
>
> The Scranton Commission said its Kent State inquiry was "especially sensitive" because it did not wish to interfere with the "criminal process" begun before an Ohio grand jury. But the circumstances under which the grand jury was convened and the men who convened it make the grand jury suspect. The Scranton report criticised Governor Rhodes for putting the Guard on campus and said it replaced the Cambodian invasion as the main focus of student discontent.

Mr. Stone's prediction that nothing would be done about the commission's reports on Kent State and Jackson State, particularly the possibility of criminal negligence on the part of the militia in Ohio and the police in Mississippi, proved, not surprisingly, to be true. Almost nine months later, the failure of the Nixon Administration to enforce the law in these two cases prompted some of the commissioners to call upon Attorney General Mitchell to act. These appeals were heard in Washington, D.C., on June 22, 1971, during a public hearing before the U.S. Senate Judiciary Subcommittee on Administrative Practice and Procedure, under the chairmanship of Senator Edward M. Kennedy.

The judiciary subcommittee was reviewing the implementation of recommendations made by Presidential and national commissions, during a series of hearings which began on May 25, 1971, with the appearance of members of the Kerner and Eisenhower commissions. On June 22 Governor Scranton appeared as the first witness to testify on the work of the President's Commission on Campus Unrest. On the subject of Kent State, Senator Kennedy referred to a memorandum dated March 19, 1971, from Assistant Attorney General Jerris Leonard to Presidential counselor Robert Finch. This memo was issued in response to Finch's inquiry regarding the status of the Justice Department's investigation into the Kent State and Jackson State killings. The following extracts are taken from the U.S. Government Printing Office transcript:

KENNEDY: And in the last paragraph, he [Leonard] said: "I am personally conducting such analysis and expect a decision with respect to the question of convening a Federal grand jury in the Northern District of Ohio to be made within the next few weeks." Before that, he indicated that they were going to follow the Attorney General's charge that all potential federal crimes be thoroughly investigated. Now, that was over 3 months ago he said this.

SCRANTON: Right.

KENNEDY: And I am just wondering whether there has been any additional communication to you as to what further action is going to be taken by the Justice Department, and whether you have any indication whether there is going to be any Federal action, and whether you do not share the belief of many others that there certainly should be.

SCRANTON: In answer to your first question, I have not had any communication with the Justice Department at all. In fact, I personally have not had any communications with them about this since October 31, when we went out of being. And to the best of my knowledge, nobody on the Commission has either . . . With regard to your last question, as to whether there ought to be a grand jury recommendation, from my knowledge of the situation at Kent State and its rigor interstices, there ought to be a Federal grand jury investigation in that area. And I have said that not only personally but many times publicly.

KENNEDY: On what do you base that?

SCRANTON: Well, I base it on primarily what we found there in our work, of course, in regard to it. Because I believe very firmly in my mind that there was enough evidence there to indicate an adjudication of whether there was a crime or not; I am not saying there was. I am simply saying that enough went on to merit an investigation by a Federal grand jury. I was frankly—this is my own personal reaction, and has nothing to do with the Commission—I was personally quite disappointed with the results of the State grand jury investigation at Kent State—not that I am trying to point a finger and saying that someone was criminal, but it seemed to me to be extraordinary, in view particularly, of the FBI investigation.

KENNEDY: Let me ask this. There isn't any follow-up by the Justice Department. Do you think it would be worthwhile to reconvene the Commission and investigate just this one question?

SCRANTON: I would think that if you were going to have a Commission for that purpose only, that it ought to be in the form of something like the Warren Commission, where you have primarily people who are legal experts. I am not, incidentally . . . But I do think that more should be done, and I hope it will.

The commission's executive director, Federal Judge Wm. Matthew Byrne, also appeared before the subcommittee and stressed the fact that the Scranton Commission had no authority to determine the guilt or innocence of any particular person. "With that limitation on the commission," he continued, "additional studies might be undertaken in that regard." He then addressed himself to the fact that almost fourteen months had gone by since the killing at Kent State, and there was still no word from the Justice Department as to their intentions:

It seems to me that the important thing at Kent and at Jackson, particularly at Kent, is that the decision should be made as to whether a grand jury is to be convened or not to be convened. And the length of time that has passed now, over a year since the incident, makes a criminal prosecution very difficult to proceed with . . .

KENNEDY: Does it take that long to conduct an investigation to satisfy the U.S. Attorney as to whether he should not prosecute? Isn't that an awfully long period of time?

BYRNE: It is a long period of time, Mr. Chairman. But there are cases that, because of the complicated nature of the facts, take that long . . .

KENNEDY: Are the facts complicated in this case?

BYRNE: In my opinion, the decision as to whether to convene a grand jury or not could certainly have been made in the time period that has passed.

At this point Senator Kennedy asked Judge Byrne whether, as a former U.S. Attorney and one who had seen the massive report of the FBI on Kent State, it would be proper for him to say whether or not he, Byrne, would have convened a federal grand jury to investigate Kent State. The judge said he would appreciate not being asked the question, whereupon Governor Scranton interjected: "I will answer; he would have."

The testimony then turned to what Kennedy called "these issues of repression and fair performance of the judiciary," a matter on which Joseph Rhodes, Jr., eloquently expressed the sentiments of many present in the Senate hearing room:

> I think the central feature of the issue of repression must remain, do we have different sets of laws in the society for different people, and will the administration use the powers of law enforcement available to it, and the system of justice to persecute and attack political opponents, people who protest in various ways, their actions, that is, the actions of the administration? I am thinking of repression in a political context; who is being repressed and why, if such a thing is going on . . . I think when people see these kind of actions by the administration, using the judicial process to attack political foes, what else can they conclude, when it has taken over a year to make a decision about the grand jury at Kent State, and the kind of actions that went on at Jackson State, what else can come to mind?

In his prepared statement for the Senate Judiciary Subcommittee, James Ahern said:

> The total silence and inactivity of the Administration in the face of a Presidential Commission's clear conclusion that grievous acts which resulted in the loss of human life were apparently committed by identifiable individuals makes its evident contempt for our more general recommendations pale into comparative insignificance.

These hearings confirmed what most Americans already know: commissions in this country, unlike their British counterparts, are often little more than a political pressure valve to be turned to whenever the going gets difficult for the Administration. They provide aggrieved citizens a forum in which to let off steam. But there is usually little intent on the part of the President to implement recommendations if they run contrary to his personal ideas. The recent reports of commissions on population growth and pornography are clear indications of this. In the case of Kent State, the Scranton Commission pointed to the need for a criminal investigation, a need that has increased as the months have gone by.

After the hearings in Washington, the Justice Department finally moved toward a decision on the convening of a grand jury. When the announcement that it would take no such action was released on August 13, commission members Scranton, Ahern, and Rhodes, Jr., expressed their "disappointment" in no uncertain terms. The following year saw the publication of Ahern's book *Police in Trouble,* in which the former police chief castigated the Nixon Administration for its handling of the commission's report and in particular for its cynical refusal to uphold the law with respect to the shootings at Kent State.

The Ohio Grand Jury

While the Scranton Commission was preparing to start its investigation, Attorney General Mitchell made a statement on July 29, 1970, which must have generated some degree of alarm in Columbus. There were "apparent violations of federal law" involving both students "and guardsmen," Mitchell said, and the Justice Department would take action with a view to prosecuting the violators "if Ohio authorities do not." It was a blunt warning to Governor James Rhodes, and coming on top of Portage County Prosecutor Ronald Kane's demands for state financial aid to launch his own grand-jury inquiry—an effort that Rhodes had thwarted because of Kane's announced determination to subpoena the governor as a witness—it left the Republican leader with no alternative. Less than a week after the Mitchell statement, Governor Rhodes announced the convening of a special Ohio grand jury to investigate Kent State. This action effectively stifled Kane and, at the same time, relieved the Justice Department of any role in the killings until after the grand jury had released its findings.

The tone and outcome of the Ohio grand-jury investigation were clear within two weeks of the convening of the jury and almost a month before the first session. "On the evidence we have available," the Attorney General of Ohio, Paul W. Brown, announced to the press, "—and we have as much as anyone—I don't see any evidence upon which a grand jury would indict any [Ohio National] guardsmen." To many, it appeared Ohio was about to conduct an inquisition and the heretics were the students, faculty, and administration of Kent State University. Those who had shot and killed would have no need to worry. Then, furthering the fears of those who doubted that the grand jury would conduct objective review of the evidence, Attorney General Brown chose Seabury Ford as one of the three state prosecutors. Ford was chairman of the Portage County Republican Party and also a former member of the Ohio National Guard's 107th Armored Cavalry, the outfit which, through its unit Troop G, had been involved in the shooting.

The other two special prosecutors chosen to present the evidence were former Allen County Prosecutor Robert Balyeat and Ravenna lawyer Perry Dickinson. On the eve of the grand-jury hearings, Balyeat stated: "This grand jury will be wide open and we are going to cover a lot of ground." Also: "I'm going to present all the evidence fairly and impartially." The Akron *Beacon Journal*, in reporting these remarks on September 13, 1970, noted that the evidence included the 8,000-page FBI report and "several thousand photographs" taken during the four-day disturbance. The evidence would also include, the newspaper pointed out, a "summary memorandum of the FBI investigation, written by the Justice Department to assist local prosecution," which "identified six Guardsmen who could face criminal charges." With an optimistic faith in American justice, the *Beacon Journal* reported: "Based on these reports and the testimony of witnesses the grand jurors could vote a variety of indictments. Possible indictments against Guardsmen might include charges of first or second degree murder, manslaughter and assault with a deadly weapon. Charges against students might include arson, malicious destruction of property, first or second degree rioting, inciting a riot and assault and battery." However real these possibilities might seem, there was little chance of a guardsman being indicted for a misdemeanor, let alone assault with a deadly weapon, when the state's Attorney General had told the jurors publicly that he knew of no evidence on which they could indict a guardsman. In the event that any of the fifteen jurors might doubt the Attorney General, there was always Seabury Ford to set them straight.

Far more witnesses appeared before the grand jury than before the Scranton Commission—especially guardsmen. Of the guardsmen on the hill subpoenaed to testify, only one of the five that the Justice Department implied might be liable to criminal charges was not summoned: SP/4 James Pierce, a Kent State student who had been activated for duty and, according to the FBI, had fired at least four times. The failure to call him to testify before the grand jury did not become significant until publication of a special edition of the Pittsburgh *Forum* devoted in part to my appeal and the possibility of a conspiracy among several of the guardsmen.

The *Forum* edition on Kent State appeared on July 30, 1971, and was prompted by the release of my *Appeal for Justice* and the fact that one of the victims, Allison, was the daughter of a Pittsburgh resident. The weekly had "dispatched five staff members to Kent, Ohio, in a search for facts which have yet to receive widespread public disclosure." Among those facts, the *Forum* reported, was the following:

> SP/4 James Pierce, a Kent student who worked at a service station near campus, dropped his rifle in a fit after firing about four shots into the crowd. Pierce, 24, who with his wife moved away from Kent because of harassment, apparently "freaked out" after the shootings.

The source of this information, the newspaper indicated, was a former army paratrooper whose mother served on the Ohio grand jury investigating Kent State. He claimed that he knew four of the five guardsmen identified by the Justice Department and said that "SP/4 James McGee and S/Sgt Barry Morris both regretted the shootings." Sergeant Lawrence Shafer, the anonymous paratrooper said, "bragged about 'taking a bead' on the student named Jeffrey Miller." Shafer is the only guardsman identified by the FBI as having shot a specific student—Joseph Lewis, Jr. Pierce's absence from the list of witnesses to the grand jury makes sense in light of the paratrooper's description of him as "the one likely to crack" before a grand jury. Pierce's whereabouts today remain a mystery.

In the two weeks preceding Governor Rhodes's convening of the grand jury, there were some startling developments. On July 22 the Ohio State Highway Patrol submitted to Portage County Prosecutor Kane a 3,000-page report on the events at Kent State. According to the Akron *Beacon Journal,* this report stated that there were "between 2,500 and 3,000 students milling on the campus during the anti-war fracas" and contained photographs "marking several hundred as 'suspects' and 'possible grand jury indictees.'" "The news media was barred" from the six-hour meeting during which highway-patrol Captain Hayh presented Kane with the massive document, the newspaper also noted. "There was no mention of sniper fire," Kane said afterward, but on the rest of the report the prosecutor had no comment.

The next day, July 23, 1970, the *Beacon Journal* revealed the contents of a brief Justice Department memorandum that summarized the principal points of the FBI report. This was not the detailed, thirty-five-page summary that Senator Young and I. F. Stone obtained in October, but it was more than enough to send a shudder of dismay through the offices of the Ohio National Guard in Columbus. The copyrighted story appeared on the front page beneath a banner headline to the effect that the Guard had faced no peril at Kent State, and prefixed it with the source of that statement: the FBI. The story itemized several key Justice Department conclusions: that there was no sniper; that the guardsmen had not been surrounded; that they could have resorted to tear gas rather than shooting; that the rock throwing had not been as widespread or as dangerous as claimed by General Canterbury; that no guardsman had been seriously injured; and, finally, that the shooting was "not proper and not in order."

The Justice Department conclusions were almost identical with those of the Knight Newspaper investigation team, whose 30,000-word report had been published in the *Beacon Journal* on May 24, 1970. Reaction in Columbus to the FBI story was highly evasive. I. F. Stone observed that "Ohio authorities did not deny the *Beacon Journal* story," but General Del Corso told newsmen the next day that the Justice Department summary failed "to include many facts which we provided." Del Corso concluded his remarks to the press by saying that "he found the FBI findings 'just unbelievable.'"

On September 13, 1970, the *Beacon Journal* published a list of 267 persons called upon to testify. Senior officials of both the National Guard and the university were subpoenaed, along with 102 students, 8 professors, 20 guardsmen, 25 policemen, 5 firemen, and 97 others. Of the National Guard officers on the hill at the time of the shooting, only General Canterbury, Lieutenant Colonel Fassinger, and Major

Jones were summoned to testify. Conspicuous once again by his absence was Captain Raymond Srp, the commander of Troop G, who had refused to appear before the Scranton Commission on the grounds that it might jeopardize his rights in the grand-jury investigation. It was he who had said immediately after the killings that the lives of his men had not been in danger and that it "was not a shooting situation."

To ensure that the testimony given to the grand jury would be secret, Portage County Common Pleas Judge Edwin W. Jones sealed off the courthouse to the news media and to anyone with cameras, tape recorders, or even artists' sketch pads. Reporters were prohibited from "loitering" in the building, and everyone connected with the hearings, including the prosecutors and witnesses, was enjoined from talking to newsmen.

On September 17 the *Beacon Journal* published an article by David Hess, of the Knight Newspapers Washington, D.C., bureau, and reporter Jeff Sallot, in which they note that Governor Rhodes had "spurned" the Scranton Commission's invitation to testify. Hess and Sallot then report that "a Portage County political figure"—a Republican—"insists Rhodes has gone to extravagant lengths to avoid testifying." This person, they go on, "says Rhodes insisted on the state grand jury action to dodge a county probe. His [Rhodes's] name was on the subpoena list for the proposed [by Kane] county grand jury investigation. When the state took over, his name went off the list."

After several weeks, during which more than three hundred witnesses testified, the grand jury settled down to decide who should and should not be indicted and to draft a report on their conclusions, a document drawn up under the guidance of the Ohio prosecutors. On the day their findings were released, October 16, 1970, Robert Boyd of the Akron *Beacon Journal* reported that President Nixon, en route to Europe, had reacted instantly and bitterly to word that Governor Scranton had implicitly criticized him for not providing "the kind of leadership needed to bring about the kind of reconciliation that we're talking about." This was, however, overshadowed by the grand-jury findings, which brought gasps of disbelief in some quarters and generated smug satisfaction in others.

The jury found that the incidents on Friday, Saturday, and Sunday—that is, May 1 through 3—constituted riots, and that the behavior of the students on Monday, the day of the shooting, was such that the noon rally "degenerated into a riotous mob." Whatever credibility this report might have had was destroyed when the jurors said: "Those who acted as participants and agitators are guilty of deliberate, criminal conduct." As for the guardsmen, the grand jury found that those who fired their weapons did so "in the honest and sincere belief and under circumstances which would have logically caused them to believe that they would suffer serious bodily injury had they not done so." No guardsman who fired, the jurors added, was "subject to criminal prosecution under the laws of this state for any death or injury resulting therefrom." Every conclusion about the Guard was contrary to the findings of the Justice Department and the FBI investigation. The jurors used such words as: "surrounded by several hundred hostile rioters"; "a constant barrage of rocks and other flying objects"; and "their supply of tear gas had been exhausted." They claimed that "photographic evidence" proved "beyond any doubt" that as the guardsmen reached the vicinity of the Pagoda "a large segment of the crowd surged up the hill, led by smaller groups of agitators approaching to within short distances of the rear ranks of the Guardsmen."

Not one of the dead was mentioned, but just about everyone except those who killed was held responsible. The grand jury condemned the "23 concerned faculty of Kent State University" for supporting and issuing, on May 3, a leaflet that deplored the burning of the ROTC but criticized the Ohio government's response to the violence. "Leadership must set the example if it is to persuade," the document affirmed, and went on to castigate Governor Rhodes for the "inflammatory inaccuracies" of his press conference on the very day the leaflet was prepared. The appeal concluded: "We call upon our public authorities to use their high offices to bring about greater understanding of the issues involved in and contributing to the burning of the ROTC building at Kent State University on Saturday, rather than to exploit this incident in a manner that can only inflame the public and increase the confusion among the members of the University community." The issuing of this appeal for conduct regulated by common sense on the part of those charged with calming down the situation, the grand jury termed "an irresponsible act."

"The major responsibility" for what had happened, the grand jury said, "rests clearly with those persons who are charged with the administration of the University." It would be inconceivable "to fix the sole blame for what happened during this period on the National Guard, the students or other participants," the jurors indicated. And:

It should be added, that although we fully understand and agree with the principle of law that words alone are never sufficient to justify the use of lethal force, the verbal abuse directed at Guardsmen by the students during the period in question [May 4, 1970] represented a level of obscenity and vulgarity which we have never before witnessed! The epithets directed at the Guardsmen and members of their families by male and female rioters alike would have been unbelievable had they not been confirmed by the testimony from every quarter and by audio tapes made available to the Grand Jury. It is hard to accept the fact that the language of the gutter has become the common vernacular of many persons posing as students in search of a higher education.

The outcome of the Ohio grand-jury investigation was predictable in that the selection of a jury from among people who resided so close to the campus naturally injected local emotionalism into their deliberations. But then, Ohio officials had not generated much confidence in their sincerity where questions of fairness and impartiality were concerned. The grand jury handed down thirty indictments "covering 25 defendants and 43 offenses." None of the twenty-five was a guardsman. They were students and non-students, and Dr. Thomas Lough, a member of the faculty. Among the indicted was the student-body president, Craig Morgan, and two of the wounded, Alan Canfora and Joseph Lewis.

On October 24, 1970, Seabury Ford, one of the three special prosecutors charged by Ohio with presenting the evidence, told Knight Newspapers reporter William Schmidt that the guardsmen "should have shot all" the troublemakers. There was "no question," he told Schmidt, that the guardsmen—Ford called them "boys"—would "have been killed up there—if they hadn't turned around and fired." The sixty-eight-year-old Republican charged that the events at Kent State were "Communist-inspired"; there can be no order in our society, he went on, "until the police are ordered to shoot to kill."

Seabury Ford's comments violated the court order prohibiting anyone connected with the grand jury from speaking publicly about the case. The callousness of his remark, however, incited Professor Glenn W. Frank to do the same. To the Akron *Beacon Journal* he said: "I speak now in contempt of court, in contempt of the naive and stupid conclusions of the special Grand Jury specifically as to their reasons for the May 4 disturbances, in contempt of Judge Jones for the gag rules placed on President White and in personal contempt for lawyer Ford for his lack of understanding after 68 years of what I believe is a wasted life." "Freedom of speech," Frank added, "is bigger than Judge Jones." Both men were cited for contempt of court, and both pleaded guilty.

The ban on comment by anyone connected with the grand jury was ordered lifted on November 3, 1970, by Federal District Court Judge Ben C. Green. Judge Green said: "Public officials may not wield an axe when a scalpel is required. . . . The events which occurred at Kent State University in the spring of this year are a matter of national, social, political, and moral concern and debate." It was the court's opinion "that when the rules on grand jury secrecy are taken into conjunction with the basic law on the right of free speech, the injunction restraining all grand jury witnesses from speaking out with reference to the comments of the special grand jury must fall as being overly broad." The ban, Judge Green charged, "prevents not only the three hundred [witnesses] from speaking, but the rest of the world from hearing."

The federal judge's decision was handed down on Election Day, and that evening, on the Walter Cronkite CBS-TV news program,

Major John Simons, chaplain of the 107th Armored Cavalry, criticized his men for having fired on the students. He pointed out to interviewer Robert Schakne that a few of the guardsmen "were angry, and so they were in a position where someone, or some, could act out their fear and anger in a very lethal way, and I think this is what occurred." In other words, Schakne asked, the Guard unit on the hill "was not a controlled, disciplined military unit?" No, they were not, Simons answered. "Somebody fired without orders."

The major also criticized Governor Rhodes, "who apparently feels that every campus disorder is another Normandy invasion," and General Del Corso's policy of permitting all guardsmen to have their weapons loaded. "There are a lot of people in Ohio who say the students had it coming," Schakne said. "If they didn't want to get shot they shouldn't have been rioting. The Guard simply did what it had to do because the men were endangered. You've heard that argument." Major Simons acknowledged that he had and said he thought "these bloodthirsty types who have never either fired or heard a shot fired in anger, I think they're very naive, hunting for a simple solution. After all, one of the tests of democracy is how much dissension it will allow and how peaceful it can keep that dissension, and I think democracy lost that round." Finally, the major was asked: "Was the situation so bad that the men had to fire?" His answer was a simple "No."

On November 9, 1970, just six days after the federal court's decision to lift the gag imposed on witnesses to the grand-jury hearings, Robert I. White spoke in Washington, D.C. The president of Kent State noted that the report of the grand jury had been "well received among the general public," but said that, in his opinion, "the Grand Jury report is inaccurate, disregarded clear evidence and, if pursued in all its nuances, would eventually destroy not only Kent State but all major universities in America." Unfortunately, Mr. White expressed far greater concern over the allegations in the grand-jury report that his administration bore a major share of the responsibility for what had happened.

The next day, November 10, Jeff Sallot of the Akron *Beacon Journal* reported that Robert Balyeat, the chief special prosecutor for the grand-jury investigation, had admitted that the fifteen jurors "never saw a Justice Department report which said there is reason to believe Guardsmen fabricated the self-defense story." This was the detailed, thirty-five-page Justice Department summary of the FBI investigation, which Senator Stephen Young of Ohio had quoted from in a speech on the floor of the Senate in mid-October and which *The New York Times* had published at the end of the month.

Sallot also reminded the public that Captain Raymond Srp of Troop G had *not* been called to testify before the Ohio grand jury, despite the fact that he was standing "among his men as they fired." It was Srp who had told Knight Newspapers reporters in May: "I didn't feel threatened and I was in the center of it." Srp's lawyer, C. D. Lambros, confirmed the fact that Srp was not subpoenaed by the grand jury, a curious omission in light of the fact that at least two people subpoenaed were not in any way involved with the events of that weekend.

More and more questions arose as to whether Balyeat and fellow prosecutor Seabury Ford had, in presenting the evidence, introduced only what was favorable to the Guard, Governor Rhodes, Mayor Satrom, and other Ohio officials. When questioned about his failure to permit the jurors to study the thirty-five-page summary, Balyeat said, "We would not normally present to the Grand Jury conclusions reached by another investigative body such as the Justice Department." This statement contradicted the earlier assurance that all the evidence available would be submitted to the grand jury. Moreover, the reports of other investigative bodies, such as the Ohio State Highway Patrol conclusions on what had happened during the four-day disturbance, were made available to the jurors.

Jury foreman Robert Hastings would only say that the jurors "had access to the FBI report." Whether they read it or not remains unclear. As for the Justice Department's critical summary of that report, Hastings refused to say whether or not it had been available. The Sallot story reported that a number of witnesses were complaining about the manner in which they were questioned by the special state prosecutors. Dr. Jerry M. Lewis, a sociology professor who in his capacity as peace marshal was in the Prentice Hall parking lot at the time of the shooting, "said that Prosecutor Balyeat asked extremely specific questions, thus preventing full explanation of what the professor saw during the shootings." Another professor, Richard Schreiber, "said the prosecutors asked no questions about his statement to the FBI that he saw a Guardsman fire a pistol over the heads of the students several minutes before the fatal volley." Sallot quoted Schreiber as saying that the grand jury "seemed to have a preconceived idea and were trying to prove it."

Apart from the three special prosecutors, particularly Seabury Ford (whose seventieth-birthday cake, according to the Akron *Beacon Journal,* was inscribed with the slogan "Shoot the Bastards" in red icing), few prominent citizens or groups had much praise for the grand jury. Speaking at Johns Hopkins University a month after the release of the jury's report, David Brinkley called it "utterly absurd." The Kent Ministerial Association and the Kent State Campus Ministries adopted a resolution criticizing the report as "an inadequate treatment of the events and eventual tragedy" and called upon the Nixon Administration to provide the American people with "a fuller explanation of these events through a Federal grand jury investigation." Senator

Young of Ohio simply called the grand jury "a fraud and a fakery," and many months later Senator George McGovern termed the Ohio investigation a "whitewash of the agents of government." Local residents, however, apparently agreed with the findings of the grand jury, according to a random sampling of sentiment taken by the Kent-Ravenna *Record-Courier* the day after those findings were disclosed.

On December 10, 1970, the Akron *Beacon Journal* reported that General Del Corso had filed the Ohio National Guard's annual report with Governor Rhodes's office. The 114-page document contained only one paragraph, less than two hundred words long, concerning the events at Kent State. The paragraph was not only brief but sweeping in its conclusion that the disturbance on the campus "ended when National Guard troops, acting in self-defense, fired their weapons, killing four students and wounding several others." The Justice Department and the Scranton Commission conclusions that the guardsmen had not fired in self-defense were completely disregarded. Although the annual report contained several photographs of Ohio guardsmen on duty at Ohio State University, there were none of Kent State. When asked about the little space devoted to what was the most controversial domestic incident of 1970, Del Corso said, "Enough has been written about Kent already. We don't want to stir it up again."

Before the end of the year, both the grand-jury report and the indictments were challenged through two civil suits filed in Federal District Court in Cleveland. One suit, filed by thirty-two professors, and another by a group of indicted students, five clergymen, and an alumnus of Kent State, overlapped in their arguments to have the court condemn as unconstitutional the grand jury's report and the indictments. On January 28, 1971, Federal Judge William K. Thomas ruled in favor of the plaintiffs with respect to the grand-jury report. By violating numerous provisions of Ohio law governing grand-jury investigations, the court ruled, and by reaching conclusions of guilt, particularly in the report's condemnation of the twenty-three faculty members for signing the statement of May 3, 1970, the jurors had exceeded their authority. Consequently, Judge Thomas found the report to be unconstitutional and ordered it expunged from the records and physically destroyed. However, the judge upheld the indictments, to the dismay of several attorneys who regarded the split decision as judicially contradictory. Former U.S. Attorney General Ramsey Clark, for one, felt it was somewhat naive to assume that the prejudice that rendered the report unconstitutional had not also affected the jury's deliberations which resulted in the handing down of twenty-five indictments, especially in view of the refusal to condemn any guardsmen.

The Thomas decision in Cleveland came just a few days before the Republican Administration in Columbus handed over the reins of power to the Democrats under Ohio's new governor, John J. Gilligan. The change-over included the retirement of Generals Del Corso and Canterbury from their respective offices as adjutant general and deputy adjutant general of the Ohio National Guard, and the immediate revision of Del Corso's policy of issuing live ammunition to guardsmen activated for civil-disturbance duty. The attorney general, Paul Brown, was also replaced, by another Brown—William—whose attitude toward Kent State differed little from that of his predecessor. Hopes that the election of a Democrat like Gilligan, a supporter of Senator Eugene McCarthy in 1968, would ensure a more thorough and impartial investigation were premature.

A month after defeating Roger Cloud, his Republican opponent, Gilligan visited Kent State University, and before a large crowd he made the following pledge for the future: "What happened in Kent last May will never happen again if I, as Governor of Ohio, can help it. No university demonstration need ever be allowed to escalate into a general riot and there will be no more students shot by Ohio soldiers attempting to reestablish civil order." But what of the past? What of the dead? Unfortunately, on that there was silence.

Despite all this, the New Year offered some prospect of intervention by the Department of Justice. Arthur Krause had been promised federal action if Ohio failed to do the job, and Ohio not only had failed but had had its efforts consigned to the incinerator by a federal judge—a decision, incidentally, that former Attorney General Paul Brown and others appealed to the U.S. Sixth Circuit Court of Appeals. Prosecutor Ronald Kane accused former Governor Rhodes of having thwarted him at every turn during the May disturbances at Kent State, and the charge could hardly be refuted since Kane's recommendation that the university be closed on Sunday, May 3, had been rejected out of hand. From within the Justice Department there were hints that the Kent State matter was under "intensive review" in light of the Ohio grand-jury report, with some indication that an announcement might be forthcoming in early spring. In Ohio, however, the prospects for action reached a new low on February 5, 1971, when Governor Gilligan challenged the authenticity of the Justice Department's summary of the FBI report. The one official document which constituted an indictment of the Ohio National Guard had become a thorn in the side of the Guard, and the new governor was persuaded to attack it. The press promptly turned to the Justice Department, which just as promptly confirmed that the summary was not only authentic but had been prepared under the supervision of Robert Murphy, then Assistant Chief of the Criminal Section of the Civil Rights Division. Time would eventually bring home to Gilligan the shoddy manner in which Ohio officials and the federal government had handled the situation, and in September 1972 he conceded that there "never had been a final decision made to pinpoint the responsibility for the tragic deaths on May 4, 1970." This concession simply recognized what others had known for almost two years: that justice had indeed been circumvented in respect to the question of who was responsible for the deaths of Allison Krause, Sandy Scheuer, Bill Schroeder, and Jeff Miller.

Two months after Gilligan's lamentable attempt to discredit the Justice Department's condemnation of the Ohio Guard's conduct, James Michener's book on the Kent State incident was published. He commented on the Ohio grand jury's report: "The gratuitous essay had these grave faults: (1) most of what was said was erroneous in that conclusions were reached contrary to the evidence; (2) it intruded upon the problems of governing a university when the members of the jury knew little about the matter and appeared to rely on the prejudices of their community; (3) the National Guard was exonerated on the basis of certain evidence when there was a mass of other evidence pointing to the fact that it shared responsibility; (4) and by prejudging the defendants in the essay, the jury seemed to be serving as both indictor and judge, thus denying the defendants their right to a fair trial." Michener quotes two reactions to the grand-jury report, both of which symbolize the political character of the response to an incident in which four young lives were lost. One, that the report was "a rural, conservative, know-nothing answer to the Scranton report, which was urban, liberal and carefully studied." The other, that the report was "a damned good Republican campaign document for the elections in November [1970]."

With the grand-jury report under federal court order to be destroyed, Ohio's attorney general delayed starting the trials of the twenty-five persons indicted. The delay stretched into months, giving rise to doubts about the strength of the evidence against the accused and the validity of the indictments. A year after the release of the report, the Kent twenty-five were still awaiting trial, partly because of attendant litigation, partly because of the state's reluctance to proceed. The Sixth District Court in Cincinnati had ruled that a trial date had to be set by no later than November 15, 1971, and Attorney General Brown complied by fixing on November 22. Some of the indicted had by now filed actions calling for the dismissal of the indictments against them. An appeal to the U.S. Sixth Circuit Court of Appeals to have the trial proceedings halted, pending outcome of other litigation against the grand jury's indictments, failed. This prompted Cleveland attorney Ben Sheerer to recommend that the Supreme Court be asked to order the trials stayed until all appeal had been heard and dealt with by the various courts involved. It was in the midst of this confusion that the U.S. Court of Appeals rejected the arguments of former Attorney General Paul Brown and upheld the

January 28 decision of Judge William Thomas that the grand-jury report be expunged and physically destroyed. The court ordered the controversial document burned within twenty-one days of handing down its decision.

Although the state of Ohio was prepared to commence the trials in September 1971, it was obvious that the attorney general's office was not eager to prosecute. The start of the long-awaited trials revealed why. Jury selection began on November 22—in the aftermath of Supreme Court Justice Potter Stewart's refusal to grant a stay—to hear the state's first case, its strongest, against Jerry Rupe, who had been indicted for arson, striking a fireman, interference with a fireman at the scene of a fire, and first-degree riot.

The trials were to take place in the Portage County courthouse at Ravenna, where the grand jury had sat and had written its diatribe against the students and faculty of Kent State University. Seven jurors were seated during the first day, two of them over the objections of defense counsel. One was William Bennett, who had signed a petition supporting the Ohio National Guard's actions on the Kent State campus. The other was Jack Ferguson, who admitted during examination that he would give more credence to the testimony of firemen and police officers than to that of other witnesses such as students. The judge who ordered the seating of Bennett and Ferguson on the jury was Edwin W. Jones, who had presided over the grand jury and the issuing of its indictments against those about to be tried in his court. Judge Jones imposed a gag rule similar to the one he had ordered in September 1970 and, in addition, banned picketing, parading, leaflet distribution, and similar protest action in the streets surrounding the courthouse. The Kent State newspaper reported in its November 23 edition that Judge Jones's order prohibited "cameras and recording devices, interviews with defense attorneys, photographs of jurors, loitering in the courthouse, statements by persons summoned as witnesses or jurors, and employees of the court from making statements and telephone calls from the courthouse." The barring of cameras did not, however, apply to local law-enforcement officers, who freely photographed, from inside the courthouse, the thirty or so people gathered outside in the snow, despite Judge Jones's order, to protest the trials.

Jerry Rupe had never been a student at Kent State University, and his presence at the scene of the burning of the ROTC building seemed to underscore the assertion that the events of that weekend were the result of an organized assault planned by outsiders and revolutionaries. This was still the local sentiment, despite the Justice Department's rejection of these assertions as unfounded and primarily based on rumor and conjecture.

The jury selection was completed on November 23, and defense

163

objections against the seating of Bennett and Ferguson were at last recognized and upheld. The two were excused. During the course of his opening statement for the defense, attorney James Hogle conceded that his client, Jerry Rupe, had interfered with firemen on the campus; therefore, this charge would not be contested. The evidence presented by special prosecutor James Primm, Jr., in connection with the remaining charges proved inadequate and the jury was unable to agree on a verdict other than the conviction of Rupe for the offense he had admitted to. The jurors had deliberated for more than eight hours. The next case presented by the state before a new jury strongly indicated that the indictments were a form of judicial persecution. Peter Bliek was charged with arson and first-degree riot in connection with the burning of the ROTC building. The first two prosecution witnesses, Howard F. Evans, Jr., a special Portage County deputy, and Steven Sivulich, director of Kent State's student-conduct program, were unable to place the accused at the scene of the crime. The next witness, Louis Szari, a graduate student on whom the prosecution relied to identify Bliek as one of two men seen throwing a gasoline-soaked cloth into the ROTC structure, was unable positively to identify the accused—at which point Prosecutor Primm admitted that the state had no more witnesses or evidence to offer, and said, "I do not wish to prosecute any further." These were the state's strongest cases. Yet they had resulted in only one conviction on one count, upon admission of guilt by the accused, Rupe. The charges against Bliek were dropped and he was released by the court.

The third case was against Larry Shub, who had been indicted for first- and second-degree riot and attempting to burn an equipment shed near the campus tennis courts on May 2, 1970. A new jury was selected to hear the case, as would be done in the trials to come. The state dropped the second-degree-riot indictment and the attempted-burning charge when Shub pleaded guilty to first-degree riot. After three trials, Ohio had obtained two convictions out of nine indictments, and both of those through admission of guilt on the part of the accused.

Lawyers for ten of the Kent twenty-five had earlier filed prejudice charges against Judge Edwin Jones, who, to his credit, agreed not to hear those particular cases, and they were assigned to Judge Albert L. Caris. On December 1, however, a similar affidavit of prejudice was filed against Caris by attorneys David Scribner and Howard Allison. This action postponed the trial of the ten defendants until the second allegation of prejudice could be heard by the Ohio Supreme Court.

Student pessimism about the manner in which the trials had begun gave way to guarded optimism, as the Kent *Stater* editorials of November 23 and December 1 dramatically demonstrated. The first opened with a call to the students to "mourn with us the death of

American justice" by going to the courthouse in Ravenna peacefully to protest Judge Jones's "circus." A week later the editorial board observed: "The fact that a jury from Portage County, that citadel of Middle America, could ignore the pressure and notoriety which accompanied the case [Jerry Rupe] and judge the facts on an impartial basis has renewed faith in one part of the system, a system functioning despite Richard Nixon and John Mitchell." The decision of Judge Jones to remove himself from the trial of ten of the defendants was encouraging, and the obviously weak position of the prosecution after only three trials gave rise to some hope that the remaining persons under indictment by the discredited grand jury would receive fair hearings.

On December 6 the state prosecutors submitted their fourth and fifth cases. Thomas G. Foglesong pleaded guilty to first-degree riot after the state informed the court that it would not prosecute him on an additional indictment of interfering with a fireman. Despite the fact that the Attorney General of Ohio had had over a year in which to prepare the cases and was prosecuting in a community recognized as being highly anti-student, he had yet to get a verdict of guilty against a defendant pleading innocent to the charges against him. This was dramatically underscored when the trial of Mary Helen Nicholas got under way before Judge Jones.

Miss Nicholas had been indicted for interfering with a fireman at the scene of the ROTC fire. The prosecution's troubles started when her defense attorney challenged the admissibility of evidence from Mrs. Ann Jacqua, the court stenographer who had recorded testimony taken by the grand jury in September 1970. The state of Ohio was reduced to trying to convict Mary on the basis of her own testimony to the grand jury that she had pulled a hose. Unfortunately, Judge Jones reverted to form and dismissed the defense argument, whereupon Mary's attorneys called for a *voir dire* examination of the witness to determine the admissibility of the state's evidence: a twenty-two-page extract of testimony before the Ohio grand jury which Mary's lawyers had never seen. The court requested Mrs. Jacqua to transcribe her shorthand notes of that particular testimony for submission the next day. At this point Judge Jones adjourned the trial. Two witnesses called earlier by the state were unable to identify Mary as being present at the ROTC fire on May 2, 1970.

The next day, December 7, 1971, Judge Jones directed the jury to return a verdict of not guilty. With the jury's acquittal of Mary Nicholas, the state's chief prosecutor, John Hayward, rose and announced that Ohio was dropping all remaining indictments.

Within the Portage County courthouse, the indictments had come to an ignominious end. Outside, in the parking lot, the grand jury's whitewash of the Ohio National Guard came to an equally ignominious end in a wastepaper basket. William Hershey, then with the Akron *Beacon Journal,* witnessed the burning of the grand jury's report. "Clerks of Courts Mrs. Lucy S. DeLeone and an aide, Mrs. Lois Enlow," he reported, "struck four matches to burn up the two official copies of the 18-page report." The circus was, at long last, over.

After a year and a half of investigations by the FBI, the Scranton Commission, the Ohio grand jury, and various local law-enforcement agencies, almost nothing had been done, either by the federal government or by the state, to pinpoint responsibility for the death of four students.

The Justice Department

The moment the M-1 rifles and .45 pistols began discharging their lethal rounds in wanton disregard of the lives of everyone in the line of fire, the constitutional rights of demonstrators, observers, and passers-by were violated. The right to peaceably assemble, as the Scranton Commission implied, was abused when the Ohio National Guard arbitrarily, and without legal authority, dispersed the May 4, 1970, rally with tear gas and bayonets. The right to due process of law and equal protection of the law was violated when guardsmen started shooting "inexcusably" into the crowd and at specific students with the apparent intent to inflict serious and grievous bodily harm. These violations have historically brought to bear the awesome powers of the Department of Justice for the purpose of ascertaining the truth through the grand-jury process. In the killing of students by police officers on the campuses of South Carolina State in 1968 and Jackson State in 1970, federal grand juries were convened. For reasons which remain officially shrouded, an exception was made in the Kent State case.

After the FBI had completed its investigation of the events at Kent State, Attorney General Mitchell made his statement that there appeared to have been violations of federal law by both students and guardsmen. This came just six days after the July 23, 1970, report in the Akron *Beacon Journal* that Justice Department lawyers in the Civil Rights Division had concluded, from the FBI report, that six Ohio National Guardsmen could be liable to criminal prosecution. At this time the head of the Civil Rights Division was Assistant Attorney General Jerris Leonard, whose position on the question of convening a federal grand jury remains uncertain today. Two subordinates, however, clearly favored intervention by the Justice Department, but neither of them could counter the attitude that prevailed among the Department's senior officers, Mitchell and Kleindienst, an attitude Richard Harris described in his book *Justice* as one in which "student radicals were regarded as an even greater threat than the forces of organized crime."

Any hope that the Civil Rights Division would fulfill its obligation to the law and to justice faded in the Justice Department's silence which followed the release of the Ohio grand-jury report. The jury's conclusions were so contrary to those of the Justice Department that there seemed little doubt that Mitchell would be compelled to convene a federal grand jury to get to the truth. The private assurance to Arthur Krause by President Nixon's adviser on domestic affairs, John Ehrlichman, that there would be "no whitewash" was promptly forgotten, however, and the weeks passed into months with nothing more substantial than repeated statements to the effect that Justice Department lawyers had the Kent State killings under intensive review.

On November 17, 1970, Carl Stern of NBC reported that the Nixon Administration was "apparently reassessing its position on the killing of four Kent State students." Stern quoted a high government law-enforcement official as acknowledging that "it would be difficult to prosecute National Guardsmen involved" in the shootings and, furthermore, that "the Administration has to give 'great weight' to the Ohio grand jury findings that the National Guardsmen acted in the face of a campus riot." Mr. Stern concluded his report:

> Attorney General Mitchell had said the government might act under the Civil Rights law if Ohio did not, but the problem is to prove that the guardsmen intended to inflict summary punishment rather than that they responded simply to fear or misjudgment. The Administration seemed today to be having second thoughts about intervening although it might have a federal grand jury review of the case.

On December 3, 1970, Jerris Leonard replied to one of my letters:

> The Justice Department has an intensive analysis of the Kent State matter now in process. Should that analysis provide us with a basis for prosecutive merit then you may feel assured that this Department will take appropriate action.

In February 1971 Arthur Krause received a letter from Jerris Leonard to the effect that the Justice Department could not reveal its intentions while legal proceedings were still pending in Ohio. This referred to the indictments handed down by Governor Rhodes's special grand jury. On April 6, 1971, Attorney General Mitchell appeared on the David Frost television program and was asked several questions about Kent State. Mitchell again brought out the self-defense story and, of all things, resurrected the old phantom sniper. The "unfortunate part of all this," he said, was that the guardsmen were just "poor kids," whom people think of as "being some heavy-handed force." The guardsmen, he repeated, are simply "a bunch of kids that are pulled out of school and their jobs and thrown into this National Guard duty and they're just like the college kids on the other side." And Mitchell asked the audience to try to understand how difficult it was for these kids when rocks were being thrown at them and they were being shot at by snipers. Frost reminded the Attorney General that all official investigations, including his own Department's, had found no evidence of snipers. Frost also reminded the Attorney General of Vice President Agnew's opinion just a few days after the killings that, if no shot was fired at the guardsmen by a sniper and the guardsmen just opened fire without a warning shot "or anything," it would be murder. At this point Mitchell said that he could not comment, because the Justice Department was still reviewing the case. Besides, Mitchell went on, "murder is a very broad term."

It was not until March 21, 1971, that segments of the religious community were alerted to the fact that the Justice Department seemed bent upon circumventing the law. Ken Clawson of the Washington *Post* sent up the Nixon Administration's trial balloon on the decision to do nothing. Clawson reported: "The government has virtually decided against convening a federal grand jury to investigate the killings of four Kent State students." Subsequent developments in Clawson's career have confirmed that his sources for the March 21 story were impeccable. He left the *Post* to become President Nixon's assistant director of communications at the White House and was later charged with having written the famous letter to a Manchester, New Hampshire, newspaper accusing Senator Edmund Muskie of an ethnic slur. Mr. Clawson's recent conduct has given rise to some wonder whether he played a role in the *Post* editorials that praised John Mitchell for his "courage" in taking the "more difficult" path of withholding action rather than convening a federal grand jury.

The Clawson story of March 21, 1971, prompted Reverend John Adams of the United Methodist Church to respond to President Nixon's admonition that moral leadership does not rest with the President alone but resides with the clergy as well. Adams alerted members of the Washington Interreligious Staff Council to the government's intention to let Kent State fade into history. A meeting with Jerris Leonard was arranged, and the group was solemnly informed that the matter was under intensive review.

On the first anniversary of the killings, Reverend Adams coordinated the release to the press of a statement by the four families of the dead students, appealing to the government for a federal grand-jury investigation: "the truth of what happened has become the fifth victim of this tragedy." These bitter parents went on to say: "It would be monstrous to deny us the judicial forum wherein the attention of the American people may be focused on the viewpoint that responsibility for the killing of our children does not rest solely upon the students, faculty and administration of Kent State." This appeal fell on deaf ears. So did a similar call for justice by Dr. Cynthia Wedel, in her capacity as president of the National Council of Churches, at a news conference on May 4, 1971, in the nation's capital.

A week later, five U.S. senators—McGovern, Hughes, Tunney, Stevenson, and Bayh—wrote to Secretary of Defense Melvin Laird, asking him for a status report on the steps taken by his department to implement the Scranton Commission's recommendation that the National Guard "never again" be issued loaded weapons when "confronting student demonstrators." The Department of Defense replied that written commitments had been received from forty-seven of the fifty states to abide by the Army field manual guidelines that had been disregarded at Kent State. The Defense Department also stated that from January 1, 1968, through June 1971 the National Guard had been called upon to assist in controlling civil disturbances on some 250 separate occasions. Only at Kent State had the Guard caused death and serious bodily injury.

On May 17, 1971, Reverend Adams and Cleveland attorney Steven Sindell met at the Justice Department with Deputy Attorney General Kleindienst. It was this meeting which prompted my writing of *Appeal for Justice* and the Board of Church and Society's decision to support my effort. The *Appeal* was submitted to the Justice Department on June 21, 1971.

We were at the time aware that the suggestion of a possible conspiracy among a few experienced guardsmen to punish the demonstrators would have as much credibility, in most quarters, as the government's allegation of a conspiracy to kidnap Henry Kissinger and blow up heating ducts had in other quarters. Nevertheless, we proceeded on that course because all investigations had failed to disclose who had started the shooting and why.

As the Justice Department indicated, "all available photographs show the Guard at the critical moments in a standing position and not seeking cover." And the Justice Department's summary of the FBI investigation is underscored by the deliberateness with which the men in the front rank are standing upright, feet firmly planted, firing their weapons at unarmed civilians who are running away from the troops, at distances from a hundred to seven hundred feet.

Three weeks after we had submitted the *Appeal* to the Justice Department, I wrote to Jerris Leonard's successor, David Norman, asking for the courtesy of a response. "I believe the Department has had more than ample time," I said, "to conduct its 'intensive analysis' of the FBI report. The Department's own summary of that report points to criminal responsibility on the part of several Ohio National Guardsmen involved in the shooting. My *Appeal for Justice* has been in your possession for over three weeks. Time is of the essence in this tragedy and it is extremely difficult to understand why the Department continues to delay announcement of its decision on the convening of a Federal grand jury in Ohio." There was no reply, not even an acknowledgment.

On July 22, 1971, the *Appeal* was made public. Congressman William Moorhead of Pennsylvania entered the text in the *Congressional Record* of that date. In doing so, he told the House: "I believe that a *prima facie* case has been made that there was murder committed at Kent State—and while I do not discount the possibility that outside agitators traveled to Kent State to add to the furor—I believe that this nation and this Congress deserve the kind of explanation that only a Federal grand jury can produce. We have a leadership crisis in this country," he continued. "Our young—and our older citizens alike—cannot take heart when it becomes apparent that Federal officials are sitting on justice because certain people might feel uncomfortable with the findings of a grand jury."

The response of the news media to the *Appeal* exceeded anything we had anticipated. Some news stories, unfortunately, implied that the report was stating as fact that guardsmen had conspired, just before the shooting, to "let the bastards have it," whereas the major thrust of the *Appeal* was a recounting of the details of May 4, 1970, with the contention that those facts strongly indicated the existence of a conspiracy. "Whatever the case may be," I said in the conclusion to the report, "these are extremely grave questions which have to be answered through the means provided by the grand jury process."

Walter Cronkite and CBS-TV News accorded the *Appeal* considerable attention on the evening of July 22 by showing several of the key photographs included in the report. John Kifner of *The New York Times* asked me what we hoped to gain in terms of the guardsmen's responsibility for the deaths. "We're not really interested in just seeing some guardsmen thrown in prison. What we're seeking is vindication —that this is not a state where a uniform is immunity."

On July 24, 1971, the Justice Department, responding to pressure by interested newsmen such as David Hess of the Knight Newspapers, indicated that "officials in the Civil Rights Division had concluded that it [the *Appeal*] contained nothing new." "The Department is absolutely correct in stating that the report contains nothing new," I said when asked for my reaction. "I am, therefore, very gratified to learn that the Justice Department is fully aware of the possibility that several guardsmen conspired together to shoot at specific students. In light of this, I am now confident the Attorney General will make the right decision." That same day the Dayton *Daily News* raised two provocative points in an editorial entitled "When Is It Appropriate for Kent State Justice?"

One—It is seriously questionable whether the Guard's commanders acted legally when they ordered their troops to break up a student rally that virtually all witnesses agree was peaceful, orderly and otherwise lawful. That decision started the events which ended with the killings of four students, the closest of whom was 270 feet from the Guard at the time.

Two—There are strong indications that some Guard members and officers knowingly gave false testimony after the tragedy in order to make it seem that their lives had been in danger. The clear and complete photographic evidence shows that the Guard was not concerned and not menaced at the time of the shooting. It seems very possible that several Guard members conspired together to develop this tale of danger. The deprivation of rights and the giving of false testimony are serious crimes. Normally, they needn't be proved but only indicated for law enforcement agencies to act. It is appalling and it is strange that the U.S. Justice Department continues to balk. Decency and the preservation of the good name of "law" itself require that such issues be met.

The New York *Post* criticized the Nixon Administration's winding down of the Kent State case and expressed the hope that the *Appeal for Justice* might "rupture the shameful silence that has enveloped" that winding-down process. In alluding to the repeated statements that the Justice Department was reviewing the case, the newspaper said: "A thorough 'review' by a federal grand jury is precisely what is and always has been called for." The editorial concluded: "It is futile to try sweeping [this case] under the rug. The ghosts of Allison Krause and her schoolmates are going to be with us for a long time."

As pressure on the Justice Department continued to mount, officials in Ohio remained silent. The state's National Guard story of self-defense had been effectively implanted in a public mind receptive to officialdom's account of what had happened because the victims were college students. This story, despite the Justice Department's findings, continued to be widely accepted, with the help of articles such as "The Guard at Kent University," written by Major General Dan Hill (Ret.), president emeritus of the State University of Wisconsin, and published in the February 1971 issue of *The National Guardsman*. General Hill faithfully followed the tone set by President Nixon the day after the deaths: if you throw a rock at combat-equipped troops, even though you might be a hundred feet away; or if you have the poor taste to yell obscenities at armed troops, even (or perhaps especially) if you are a female—then you must not be surprised if you are shot. The general put it somewhat more romantically: "Jeffrey G. Miller and Allison B. Krause [265 and 343 feet away, respectively] were 'courting fickle fame at the mouth of a cannon.' " Sandy Scheuer's death, he concedes, "was the most tragic of all," because she was not demonstrating. But, he says (erroneously), she was "the only person thereabouts who was en route to a scheduled class." Needless death, especially when the victims are young, "fills one with regret," Hill goes on, and then compares the killing of the four students with accidents in laboratories or on the highway. The general leans heavily on the discredited Ohio grand-jury report and refers only two times to the Scranton Commission report and not at all to the Justice Department's summary of the FBI investigation.

Not surprisingly, he brings up the sniper story, in spite of the Justice Department report that the "FBI has conducted an intensive search and has found nothing to indicate that any person other than a guardsman fired a weapon." General Hill does not say flatly that there was a sniper, but he manages to convey the impression that there was, despite all official statements to the contrary. "Learned and experienced Doctors of Medicine," he states, are "in disagreement as to whether one of the wounded students was hit by a non-military bullet." No identification is made of these "Doctors of Medicine," but they are Joseph W. Ewing, Milton Helpern, Joseph Davis, Robert Sillary, and three army physicians at the Walter Reed Medical Center. General Hill is referring to Dr. Ewing's statement that Donald MacKenzie's wound had "certainly not" been inflicted by "a missile from an M-1 rifle or a .45 pistol." The general does not mention Dr. Ewing's connection with friends of the top brass of the Ohio National Guard. Dr. Ewing is a plastic surgeon who resided in Akron at the time and was, as reported by the *Beacon Journal,* a personal friend of Akron's police chief, Harry Whiddon, who was a golfing companion of Generals Del Corso and Canterbury. Moreover, it was Whiddon's aide, Frank E. Mianowski, who "witnessed [Ewing's] statement," as also reported in the *Beacon Journal,* that MacKenzie's wound was "non-military." This connection of itself would not necessarily cast doubt on Dr. Ewing's credibility. However, the fact that Drs. Helpern, Davis, and Sillary disagree with Ewing, and that the three army doctors, including Lieutenant Colonel Norman Rich, were unable to agree or disagree with him does.

Dr. Helpern told the Scranton Commission that MacKenzie's wound "definitely could have been caused by .30 caliber ammunition and that he could not rule out that it had been caused by .45 caliber ammunition." It seems reasonable to assume that Dr. Helpern, during his many years of service as chief medical examiner of New York City, has had much more experience in the field of gunshot wounds than a plastic surgeon from Akron, Ohio. Dr. Sillary, the Akron *Beacon Journal* of May 24, 1970, reported, "pointedly disagreed" with Joseph Ewing. "It is entirely possible," Dr. Sillary told the newspaper, "for an M-1 bullet to cause a clean through-and-through wound without extensive damage." Dr. Sillary is not a plastic surgeon but a forensic pathologist in Detroit. Dr. Joseph Davis, chief medical examiner of Dade County in Florida, also rejected Dr. Ewing's assertion that the absence of extensive damage to MacKenzie proved that the wound was not caused by military ammunition. Dr. Davis, the *Beacon Journal* said, "suggested the bullet that struck MacKenzie may have passed through another person first." That person might have been Sandy Scheuer, who also received a through-and-through wound, which proved fatal.

I have explored here in detail the myth surrounding Donald Mac-Kenzie's wound to demonstrate the extent to which one has to probe in the Kent State killings just to get at the truth about one seemingly unimportant aspect of the event. Also, articles like General Hill's contain the foundation stone of the Guard's explanation for what happened and why. The general paints a terrifying picture of May 4, 1970, calling the incident "the Battle of Blanket Hill." "Well-disciplined strikers in unlawful assembly at a factory gate," he says, "are not the same as wild-eyed students completely organized and led to planned chaos"—an allusion to the Cleveland truckers' strike, in which several guardsmen fell injured and were shot at. But "public opinion," General Hill writes at the end of his article, "is in favor of the Guardsmen at Kent."

Before the release to the press of my *Appeal for Justice,* a number of congressmen and women joined together in a letter calling upon Attorney General Mitchell to convene a federal grand jury. Initiated by William Moorhead and Charles A. Vanik (D-Ohio), the letter said that only such a jury "can provide the kind of information necessary to satisfy the many doubts that surround the tragic event which occurred at Kent State." Those who concurred by signing were Shirley Chisholm, Bella Abzug, Herman Badillo, Jonathan Bingham, Seymour Halpern, Edward Koch, Bertram Podell, Benjamin Rosenthal, James Scheuer, and William Ryan, all of New York; Don Edwards and Thomas Rees of California; Michael Harrington of Massachusetts; David Obey of Wisconsin; Edwin Forsythe of New Jersey; and Louis Stokes of Ohio. Mitchell did not acknowledge receipt of the letter, an omission which prompted Congressman Moorhead to accuse the Attorney General of holding members of the House of Representatives "in contempt," and to assert that his silence implied that he condoned the shooting and its consequences.

At the end of July 1971, Congressman Moorhead sought to examine the FBI report for himself. At first, Justice Department lawyers proposed that the congressman be briefed on the substance of the report, but later even that offer was withdrawn. It seemed to Moorhead that the Nixon Administration had decided it was politically wiser to "sweep the Kent State incident under the rug." On July 30, James Wechsler of the New York *Post* asked: "How long will the Senators and Congressmen who have pressed for Justice Department action wait before initiating a full-scale inquiry of their own?" The same day, in Washington, Senators Hart, Kennedy, Bayh, and Tunney wrote a long letter to David Norman, then acting head of the Civil Rights Division, asking questions in connection with his nomination as permanent replacement for Jerris Leonard. As members of the Senate Judiciary Committee, the four senators were particularly interested in Norman's attitude toward equal rights. At the conclusion of their letter, they said, "We are also concerned about the Department's failure even to reach a determination on the convening of a federal grand jury in connection with the Kent State tragedy nearly fifteen months after the killings occurred, and our questions cover that matter as well." Those questions were:

1. Why had no decision been reached prior to March 19, 1971,* about an incident which occurred in May 1970?
2. As to the four and one-half months since March 19, 1971, could you provide us with a description of what has occurred within the Department on this matter and the reasons for the continuing delay? If any staff or Division-level recommendations have been made, when were they given and what has happened to them?
3. What is the present status of the Kent case and when can we expect a final decision?
4. Are you satisfied with the course the Kent case has taken in the Civil Rights Division and the Department? Do you feel such delay is a sound policy from the point of view of confidence in the integrity of our system of legal justice?

Surprisingly, Mr. Norman wrote back two days later, and inadvertently disclosed that Deputy Attorney General Kleindienst had misled Reverend John Adams and attorney Steven Sindell at their May 17 meeting, when Kleindienst assured them that no recommendation on Kent State had been made by the Civil Rights Division and for that reason Kleindienst arranged another meeting for Adams with David Norman. In his reply to the four senators, Norman said: "In March 1971 Mr. [Jerris] Leonard made his recommendation to the Attorney General." We had suspected that this was the case but had no alternative but to proceed on the assurances of Kleindienst that the Kent State case was still under review. Consequently, the *Appeal for Justice* was written and submitted *after* the Civil Rights Division had made a decision and passed it on to Mitchell.

David Norman told the senators that he "had played no role in the evaluation of the materials or the recommendations made before that time [March 1971]." He said that, after he succeeded Leonard, "the Attorney General asked me to study the case and to give my views as well. I have been studying the case but, obviously, because of the overall pressure of the work of the Civil Rights Division, I have not

---

* The date of Jerris Leonard's letter to Robert Finch on Kent State.

been able to devote as much time to it as I would have liked." At this point Mr. Norman claimed that he had "become familiar with the results of the investigations, including some 8,000 pages of reports," a statement he would completely reverse almost a year later when faced with demands by representatives of the 50,000 student petitioners for a federal grand jury. To the students, David Norman said he was *un*familiar with the Kent State material.

As for the *Appeal,* Norman's letter provided us with the only official acknowledgment that the Justice Department had the document and had apparently read it. "I have met with representatives of the families of the students involved," he wrote, "who in June delivered to me the report of Peter Davies on this incident. Thereafter, I instructed staff attorneys to study the Davies report carefully to determine whether any new leads were disclosed that would affect a prosecutive decision. Since that time I have provided the Attorney General with a summary of the report and its relationship to the information previously available to us, and on July 30, 1971, I gave the Attorney General my recommendation. The Attorney General is studying the matter and he has advised me that he expects to announce a decision soon."

If nothing else, we had at long last compelled Attorney General Mitchell to make public a decision apparently reached five months earlier. Officially, of course, Justice Department spokesmen continued to tell newsmen that no such decision had been made, because "the Kent State question is still under review." Trudy Rubin of the *Christian Science Monitor* reported on August 5 that the Justice Department's position was that no decision would be announced before Congress recessed. To questions on the matter of timing, Miss Rubin quotes an official who states that the anticipated statement "will be made at the appropriate time notwithstanding whether Congress is in session."

On August 3, 1971, the executive head of the Department of Social Justice of the National Council of Churches, Father Robert Chapman, released the contents of a letter he had written calling upon Attorney General John Mitchell to convene a federal grand jury. "Unless the protracted silence of your office is speedily corrected by the establishment of a panel of inquiry," Father Chapman said, "your Department's professions of concern are to be branded insincere, and the Department of Justice, under your leadership, will seem to be dilatory in pursuing justice, if not actually to be protecting injustice." A week later, the *Christian Science Monitor* criticized the anticipated Justice Department decision to do nothing. In an August 10 editorial the newspaper said: "There is some expectation in Washington that after Congress is comfortably away for its summer recess the U.S. Department of Justice will announce that there will be no federal grand jury investigation of the shootings at Kent State University. Failure to pursue that ultimate stage of investigation of a heartbreaking tragedy would leave an open wound on the American conscience."

The "crux of the matter," the *Monitor* editorial went on to point out, is "whether there had been any kind of concerted decision by the members of the Ohio National Guard to wheel and fire" at the demonstrators. The reputation of the Guard units involved, the newspaper argued, "would justify" a thorough federal investigation to determine whether or not there is evidence to substantiate the allegations of criminal misconduct. "If there is no evidence of a concerted decision it should clearly be made known. If there was such a decision it should be probed and probably prosecuted." The Ohio grand-jury investigation having been totally discredited, this "leaves the legal process badly incomplete," the *Monitor* asserted, and concluded: "If the purpose of the administration, which can be readily understood, is to encourage public opinion to forget about Kent State, it will be ill-served by such a decision."

On Friday, August 13, a radio station in Ohio reported that Attorney General Mitchell was going to announce his decision on Kent State before the end of the day. John Adams called me around 3:30 in the afternoon and said, "It's coming today and it's no." There is no denying the mixed emotions of anger and despair which washed through me at that moment. Not only was the Attorney General failing to uphold his sworn obligation to our Constitution and laws, but like a child caught with his hand in the cookie jar, he was squirming out of that obligation with the ridiculous excuse that he couldn't help it because there was insufficient evidence to warrant the convening of a grand jury. The decision was released at 4 P.M. on a Friday, with Congress safely out of town.

For the parents, particularly those who had not yet lost faith in their government, the decision was a bitter blow. Of everyone who for sixteen months had been involved in the effort to persuade the government to fulfill its promises to enforce the law, Arthur Krause was probably the only one among us who did not harbor even a tiny hope that the decision would be favorable. Yet he was the driving force which sustained our commitment. Mitchell's decision did not mean the end for us. On the contrary. August 13, 1971, marked the end of a chapter and the beginning of another. If the federal government was determined to circumvent the law, then Congress must be persuaded to use its investigatory powers to search out the truth about Kent State.

In his statement, John Mitchell conveniently ignored the violation of the victims' civil rights, Section 242 of the U.S. Code, Title 18, by claiming that there was "no credible evidence" of a conspiracy on the part of guardsmen. Without the convening of a federal grand jury to probe for that evidence, Mitchell's claim was both misleading and a pointed expression of contempt for the law.

Although Mitchell conceded that the gunfire was "unnecessary, unwarranted and inexcusable," he claimed that the Justice Department could do nothing further, because, as he put it, "there is no likelihood of successful prosecution of individual guardsmen." The most that the government could do, he went on, was "hope that any type of recurrence can be avoided by this experience and that incidents like this will never again be part of our national life." As if these remarks were not enough, the Attorney General then asserted that the Department had "taken every possible action to serve justice." But, apart from the FBI investigation and the Civil Rights Division's analysis of that probe, the Justice Department had done absolutely nothing to serve the interests of justice. Mitchell's statement was a cruel insult to our intelligence and that of the public, which was still very much in the dark about what really had happened at Kent State on May 4, 1970.

Reverend Adams once again had the unhappy task of coordinating the release of a statement by the parents of the dead students. "The shock of learning of the decision of the Department of Justice not to convene a federal grand jury is nearly as great as the shock that came to us when our children were killed." The parents had believed that the judicial branch of the American democratic process "would be activated and would show clearly the wrong that was done, and would identify those who were responsible for its having happened."

Reverend Adams told the press: "It is difficult to reconcile the fact that the shootings were inexcusable—meaning there are no excuses that can be made for them—and the denial that the National Guard, whether individual guardsmen or command officers, can be held responsible for them. There is an inconsistency in this statement of the Attorney General that is of considerable dimension." Asked about the possible conspiracy in the shooting, which the *Appeal for Justice* had brought up, Adams replied: "There can be no final determination of this until sworn statements are taken from the National Guardsmen and their officers. In the meantime, the evidence points toward such a pre-arranged and concerted action."

As to Mitchell's comment that further investigation by the Justice Department "would not be warranted," Reverend Adams responded: "One would think that it was reasonable to search with every instrument available to the Department of Justice in order that no scrap of evidence would be missed," particularly in a case where people had been killed through "such a misuse of military power by a government against its own citizenry."

In Ohio, the new adjutant general of the state's National Guard,

Dana Stewart, expressed satisfaction with Mitchell's decision, which he called "fair." A federal grand jury, he asserted, "was unnecessary." He had nothing to say, of course, about the government's condemnation of the guardsmen for inexcusably shooting at the students. Craig Morgan, former Kent State student-body president, protested: "I think it is morally absurd that after four students were killed and nine wounded no official action of any kind has been taken against anyone who pulled a trigger." It was now all too clear, Morgan's successor, Bill Slocum, bitterly observed, that as far as Mitchell and the Nixon Administration were concerned, "law and order will be applied *against* blacks and students and certainly not *for* blacks and students."

Scranton Commission member James Ahern expressed dismay at the Mitchell announcement. "It is precisely the kind of action that continues to undermine confidence in our criminal justice system," he said. Ahern also said he was not really surprised by the decision not to do anything, because, he believed, it was "politically motivated," a conviction shared by many that weekend. Robert Hocutt, one of the Justice Department attorneys involved in studying the FBI report, had left the Civil Rights Division before Mitchell's announcement and was free to comment: "I don't see how he [Mitchell] can agree the shootings were inexcusable and then conclude there was no hope for successful prosecution. That's a lousy basis for deciding not to prosecute anyway." The former chief prosecutor for the Ohio grand jury had the gall to say that Mitchell's decision corroborated the work of the state grand jury, and Seabury Ford told newsmen the decision "meets with my approval." The foreman of that jury, Robert Hastings, was much more cautious in his comment. "I assume," he said, "that the Attorney General's department has determined that no federal laws were violated." As expected, everyone in Ohio connected in an official capacity with what had happened breathed a sigh of relief. There were also a few others, such as former Kent State president Robert White, who agreed.

Editorial comment, however, was generally critical, sometimes confused, and, in the case of the Washington *Post,* misguided. Mitchell's decision, the *Christian Science Monitor* predicted, "will likely haunt the Nixon Administration for a long time to come." Had the Attorney General better served the interests of justice by convening a federal grand jury, the newspaper contended, such an act could have been a sign of the Administration's "desire to pursue the interests of youth as soberly as it defends the established system." The editorial went on: "Among the younger generation of new voters, as well as the many adults who identified with the parents of the slain youths, the feeling will persist that the Justice Department has backed off the Kent State case to avoid digging up the Administration's own sorry comments on the case—remarks which now must go as unredeemed as the allegations about the Ohio National Guard must go unproved."

On August 16 the New York *Post* editorialized: "There is, lamentably, scarcely any reason to believe that the Attorney General's review was confined strictly to the evidence or that his expressions of regret are genuine. Washington's political manhandling of this tragedy from the first was shamefully evident. Nor is there much consolation for anyone in Mitchell's expression of 'hope' that there will not be another Kent State." The Akron *Beacon Journal,* addressing itself to Mitchell's conclusion that further action by the Justice Department was unwarranted, said, "This is a great responsibility for the Attorney General to take, particularly in view of the opinion of other informed persons that the evidence should be presented to a grand jury." The newspaper confessed to having had mixed feelings about the advisability of convening a federal grand jury, but concluded: "In retrospect, it appears that a federal grand jury might profitably have picked up the investigation where the state grand jury left off in October 1970."

Two days later, on August 18, *The New York Times* agreed that Mitchell was "probably right in contending that the chances of proving personal guilt against any guardsmen are virtually nil." Incredibly, the *Times* suggested that Mitchell "might have served the cause of fair-minded leniency by recommending that the case against the [twenty-five indicted] students be dropped as well." In other words the *Times* was proposing to balance the scales of justice: Don't prosecute anyone for committing arson and harassing firemen as a fair exchange for not proceeding against anyone for causing four deaths.

The Washington *Post* editorial comment on Mitchell's decision came in two parts, the first on August 18 and the second on August 26, and throughout, one could not help but get the impression that they had been written by the White House or, possibly, by the Justice Department itself. Mitchell, the *Post* contended, lacked "the jurisdiction to do what ought to be done"; but he "demonstrated a bit of courage by taking the harder of the two roads open to him." On August 26, the paper proclaimed that it was going "to set the record straight on why federal prosecutions in situations of this kind are rare—and why we thought Mr. Mitchell was probably right." It acknowledged that the FBI investigation, the Scranton Commission's report, and even Mitchell's condemnation of the shooting provided substantial support for the view "that some crimes were committed by Guardsmen at Kent State." However, the newspaper continued, it is unlikely that these are crimes "over which the federal government has jurisdiction." Sections 241 and 242 of the U.S. Code, Title 18, exist to provide the federal government with the jurisdiction to intervene in incidents like Kent State, just as the government had intervened in the Jackson State killings and the 1968 killings on the campus of South Carolina State College. But the *Post,* in setting the record straight, solemnly informed its readers that in cases such as Kent State and Jackson State "there are only three federal criminal statutes which can possibly be applied and each of them is fairly narrow in scope." Two of the three are Sections 241 (Conspiracy) and 242 (Civil Rights). The three statutes, as defined by the *Post,* are:

> One punishes persons, such as Guardsmen, who deprive anyone of federally protected rights because of race or because he is an alien . . .
>
> Another punishes persons who interfere with the exercise of a long list of individual rights, such as voting, serving on a jury or participating in a federal program . . .
>
> The third punishes those who engage in a conspiracy to deprive citizens of federal rights . . .

The first is a distorted paraphrase of Section 242 of the U.S. Code, one law possibly violated by the six guardsmen identified by the Justice Department as having "fired into the crowd or at a specific student," by their own admission to federal investigators. The *Post,* however, following its own erroneous version of Section 242, said that it "simply didn't apply at Kent State since both the Guardsmen and the students were white citizens." The *Post* editorial staff was in effect saying that this federal statute applied only to blacks or foreigners.

The third statute referred to is Section 241. The *Post* claimed that this was the only statute "that could have been invoked at Kent State." There was, however, nothing that Attorney General Mitchell could do about it, because, as the *Post* put it, "there was insufficient evidence of conspiracy to justify further action" by the Justice Department. The *Post* does not say how it reached such a conclusion without any evidence having been obtained through a grand jury. As long as this tool for obtaining testimony goes unused, there may well be insufficient evidence of a conspiracy, but the lack of such information need not preclude the government from convening a federal grand jury to ensure that no stone has been left unturned and the interests of justice are served.

"It is grossly unfair to blame Mr. Mitchell for not prosecuting the Guardsmen for murder or manslaughter," the *Post* editorial concluded. But none of us blamed Mitchell for not prosecuting guardsmen. Like the *Post,* we could not know exactly what had transpired among the men during their stay on the football practice field and their march up the hill to the Pagoda. We blamed Mitchell for not using the tools available to him, the tools he had used in the Jackson State killings and, with impressive swiftness, in the government's prosecution of Daniel Ellsberg, the Berrigans, Sister Elizabeth McAllister, and Leslie Bacon.

The following day Reverend Adams, Dr. Dean Kelley of the National Council of Churches, Rabbi Richard Hirsch of the Union of American Hebrew Congregations, and Mr. Robert Jones of the Washington Interreligious Staff Council joined together to take the editor of the Washington *Post* to task for not only failing "to set the record straight" but setting it "further askew." The article, they wrote, "inaccurately sets forth the law and incorrectly interprets it." Pointing to the editorial's rejection of federal jurisdiction on the grounds that the guardsmen and the students were white, the four religious leaders said: "This is a misreading of Title 18, U.S. Code, Section 242, which states that 'Whoever under color of any law, statute, ordinance, regulation, or custom wilfully subjects *any* inhabitant of any state . . . to the deprivation of any rights, privileges, or immunities secured or protected by the Constitution or laws of the United States, *or* to different punishments, pains or penalties, on account of such inhabitant being an alien, or by reason of his color, or race, than are prescribed for the punishment of citizens, shall be fined . . . etc.' The editorial writer misinterpreted the conjunction 'or' and assumed that Section 242 would only apply if the students and Guardsmen had been of different races."

The four men went on to observe that the *Post* had gone further than Mitchell in seeking to place the dead of Kent State beyond the pale of both the Constitution and federal laws. "He [Mitchell] asserted that 'there is no likelihood of successful prosecutions of individual guardsmen.' He did not say that the federal code was inapplicable." Even if some guardsmen had committed murder or manslaughter, the editorial had claimed, these are crimes which "in our federal system are left in the hands of state governments with some minor and specific exceptions."

As for the *Post*'s statement that the applicable statutes are "fairly narrow in scope" and cannot be invoked in the case of Kent State, the letter called upon the newspaper to refer "to a release of the Department of Justice for Wednesday, May 19, 1971, in which the Attorney General announced that indictments were returned against police officers in Boston and in Savannah for depriving citizens of their civil rights. A specific reference is made to the case of a policeman, Wadsworth W. Sears of Willacoochee, Georgia, who was charged with having allegedly shot and killed a *white* farmer, Carrol McKinnon, on October 20, 1969. The release states clearly in reference to the cases cited that 'All indictments charge a violation of Title 18, United States Code, Section 242, which carries a maximum penalty of one year in prison and a $1,000 fine.' "

Finally, the four religious leaders referred to Section 245 of Title 18, subparagraph (2), which states: "Nothing in this subsection shall be construed to limit the authority of federal officers, or a federal grand jury, to investigate possible violations of this section." The word "possible," the writers felt, was the "key word in the appeals that have been made" to the Nixon Administration generally and to the Attorney General in particular.

The Washington *Post* did not acknowledge receipt of this letter.

Even as *The New York Times* and the Washington *Post* were agreeing with Mitchell that nothing could be done, the Akron *Beacon Journal* on August 17 published an anonymous letter from an Ohio National Guardsman which expressed thoughts and opinions one would have expected from those two giants of journalism. "With so many unanswered questions surrounding the four murders at Kent State to burden the American conscience," the guardsman wrote, "I find it almost incomprehensible that the U.S. Attorney General could close the official books on the May 4 tragedy while paradoxically agreeing with previous investigations that the shooting deaths were 'unnecessary, unwarranted and inexcusable.' " He went on to ask how four inexcusable "murders," whether or not they were premeditated, could be "locked away in a virtual vacuum of suspended legal animation? This hypocritical action is tantamount to admitting we live in a police state where having a uniform gives one the legal right to take a life in the name of law and order without any semblance of due process or legal recrimination." His words eloquently expressed what we all felt in the aftermath of Mitchell's announcement. The rest of the letter bears inclusion here if only to point up the contrast with the comments of others.

> As a Guardsman who was present at Kent State, I cannot wholly dismiss the possibilities of a deadly collusion. Just as I know many Guardsmen who were appalled by the murders, I know others who welcomed the deadly confrontation.
>
> Guardsmen are no more than a representative cross-section of the society in which they live. We share the same prejudices, resentments, life styles, philosophies, neuroses, and politics as our non-uniformed peers. We are minimally trained in military proficiency and virtually untrained in the discipline and personal restraint so necessary for critical civil duty.
>
> Guardsmen share one common denominator—we have successfully avoided real military duty—and the wearing of a Guard uniform does not insure rational action any more than the wearing of bell bottoms, beads, and peace buttons insures irrational action.
>
> I sincerely hope that our sword of "justice" is not single-edged, operating only on behalf of the State, and that the American Civil Liberties Union is successful in pursuing the truth. For only when armed with the truth can we hope to avoid future Kent States and Jackson States.

In response to this admirable letter, we appealed in turn to any guardsman who might have information to divulge provided it could be done with a valid assurance of anonymity. Dr. Dean Kelley and Father Robert Chapman of the National Council of Churches agreed to accept any such information, and, on August 27, the *Beacon Journal* published my letter. I began by referring to the anonymous letter of the seventeenth and to the fact that Mitchell's decision "has denied this Guardsman, and others, the judicial forum in which they would feel free to reveal whatever they may know about May 4. Such a forum is a federal grand jury with its power to utilize the immunity statute to protect witnesses from self-incrimination. Mr. Mitchell's refusal to use this instrument for securing the truth has driven witnesses, like this Guardsman, to speak out anonymously through your newspaper. It is difficult to imagine anything more bizarre in our legal history."

I offered the assurance that whatever information was given Dr. Kelley and Father Chapman "will not be divulged to any lawyers and their clients who are, or may become, involved in civil actions stemming from the tragedy unless permission to do so is given in writing." I explained that any statements offered would be used solely "for the drafting of another appeal to Attorney General Mitchell without identification of individuals, if requested, to reconsider his decision." There was, unfortunately, no response, but the letter did move the writer of the August 17 letter to get in touch with Reverend Adams. This led to my having several long conversations with him about May 4, 1970, and, later, to his willingness to identify himself as Michael Delaney.

Delaney, a former sergeant in the Ohio National Guard, was not on the hill at the time of the shooting, but he did have a great deal to say about an unusual incident that occurred just before the gunfire, an incident that the Justice Department and the Scranton Commission had both noted with cursory interest and the Ohio grand jury had completely ignored. The incident involved a twenty-two-year-old man, officially described as a freelance photographer, who, apparently, was not a regular student at Kent State but was enrolled for a special course. One of his major activities on campus was taking photographs of participants in rallies and demonstrations, and his employer, it is now believed, was either the FBI or the campus police department. On May 4, 1970, he was engaged in this activity, as noted in photograph 2 in this book. What he did just before, during, and after the shooting, however, remains unclear, and no effort has been made either by federal or by state investigators to explore his actions. For example, we still do not know why this man was the only civilian on the campus that day known to have been armed with a pistol. The Justice Department avoids the question in its summary of the FBI report:

> Finally, there is no evidence of the use of any weapons at any time in the weekend prior to the May 4 confrontation; no weapon was observed in the hands of any person other than a Guardsman, with the sole exception of Terry Norman, during the confrontation. Norman, a freelance photographer, was with the Guardsmen most of the time during the confrontation. A few students observed his weapon and claim that he fired it at students just prior to the time the Guardsmen fired. Norman claims that he did not pull his

183

weapon until after the shooting was over and then only when he was attacked by four or five students. His gun was checked by a Kent State University policeman and another law enforcement officer shortly after the shooting. They state that his weapon had not been recently fired.

It is curious that the Justice Department should disregard the obvious questions which arise from this reference to Terry Norman. We are not informed whether Norman was interrogated by the FBI, as were many students and professors, nor are we told why he was permitted to carry a gun in such a volatile situation. How is it that this student was able to move freely about the campus with the Ohio National Guard? What was his role in the shooting, if any? The Scranton Commission tells us even less about Norman's behavior:

> A free-lance photographer was taking pictures of the demonstration and was seen with a pistol after the Guard fired. Several civilians chased him from Taylor Hall into the Guard line, where he surrendered a .38 caliber revolver. The gun was immediately examined by a campus policeman, who found that it had not been fired.

Sergeant Delaney was the first person to confront Norman after the shooting and took possession of Norman's .38 pistol. But the Kent State police quickly intervened and took the gun from him. Like the Justice Department, the Scranton Commission avoided asking what Norman was doing with the weapon in the first place, and no official report mentions whether or not the FBI examined Norman's gun. The word of a campus policeman can hardly be accepted as proof positive that Norman had not fired his pistol, but that is what we are expected to accept without question. Delaney is convinced that Norman's weapon *was* fired, and so is an NBC newsman, Fred de Brine, who witnessed Norman's arrival at the Guard's line near the ruins of the ROTC building and his surrender of the .38 to a guardsman, who passed it over to the campus policeman mentioned by the Justice Department.

The reason that both Michael Delaney and Fred de Brine of NBC believe that Norman's gun had been fired was indicated by the former sergeant when he described what happened at the time Norman ran back to the Guard's line near the burned-down ROTC building. Delaney says that when Norman arrived at the line Delaney and de Brine heard him say several times, "I had to shoot!" "They would have killed me," Delaney quotes Norman as telling those present—"they" presumably being students who knew of his undercover activities for the campus police. Even more impressive in Delaney's mind is the fact that the first Kent State policeman to handle Norman's .38 pistol said, according to the former guardsman, "My God! It's been fired."

The Akron *Beacon Journal,* in its Pulitzer Prize story on the Kent State case, reported on May 24, 1970, that film "showed a man clutching a briefcase chasing him [Norman], yelling, 'Stop that man! He has a gun! He fired four shots!' Norman, 22, who for three years had taken identification photographs of campus activists for campus police, denied firing." The report also identified the campus policeman who examined Norman's gun as Tom Kelley and quoted him as saying that the gun was "fully loaded" and "had not been fired."

Eszterhas and Roberts quote sophomore Gene Pekarik as saying that he saw "a student in a sport coat running around near Blanket Hill 'like a wildman.' " The student was Norman, and Pekarik claimed he was so close he "could see the gold bullets in the chamber." Eszterhas and Roberts also questioned Norman. He told them: "I was up on the hill after the shooting and I stopped to help one of the students who'd been hit and some of them surrounded me and yelled, 'Get the pig! Get the pig!' " He alleged that one of the students harassing him reached for a knife, and then he, Norman, drew his .38 and "scared" the student away.

Another witness was Major John Simons, of the 107th Armored Cavalry, who saw Norman surrender the gun. Michael Delaney told me that at the time Norman appeared to him to be extremely agitated. This guardsman believes that Norman was working for the FBI on May 4, 1970, a not unusual occupation for students on campuses while John Mitchell was Attorney General. The basis for Delaney's conviction that Norman was working for the FBI on May 4, 1970, is that he was told this by a Kent State University official. The former sergeant's task that day was the issuance of National Guard press passes to accredited newsmen. Norman himself first asked Delaney for such a pass, but when he could not produce credentials substantiating his status as an accredited newsman, his request was denied. Some minutes later, Delaney told me, a member of the Kent State Public Information Office requested a pass on Norman's behalf and told the sergeant it was all right to issue one, as Norman could be vouched for by the university. This was not enough for Delaney, however. He insisted that passes could be given only to members of the press with proper credentials. It was then, Delaney says, that a Kent State official intervened—he believes it was an officer of the campus police department—and told the former guardsman that the pass had to be issued. Delaney quotes the official as saying to him that Norman was "under contract to the FBI to take pictures" of the demonstrators. This, according to Michael Delaney, is how Terry Norman got his National Guard press card.

James Michener notes that Norman was "rumored to have been hired by the FBI and the campus police to photograph disturbances. (Later the FBI denied that he had worked for them.)" Michener also confirms that Norman's gun was "retrieved within minutes by the campus police, who examined it and reported, 'It was not fired.' " But too many disclosures about undercover surveillance of students and instances of individuals acting as provocateurs while engaged on behalf of the FBI or local law-enforcement agencies have undermined the credibility of such denials. Michener quoted the reaction of some students to the denials: " 'The police lied. Norman did fire the first shot, as he had been ordered to do. They're covering up for their boy.' " Michener reports that Harriet Wolin, a sophomore, was "in a position to see what happened" and told him: "The photographer [Norman] pulled a gun out of his jacket and struck a friend of mine on the side of the head. Shortly after that the guardsmen opened fire." Why Michener did not pursue this matter further is not explained. Certainly, several intriguing questions arise that, to my knowledge, no one has bothered to explore.

Norman was the only student who was known to be armed with a gun on May 4, 1970. We have a witness who saw Norman running around "like a wildman" waving that gun. Surely such bizarre behavior would provide Generals Del Corso and Canterbury with a perfectly reasonable excuse for the shooting: their men saw Norman and believed he was about to fire at them. Yet the generals and the Ohio special prosecutors to the grand jury totally ignored Terry Norman, his gun, and the witnesses. Why? The Ohio National Guard could have arrested Norman after the shooting, but they did not. They simply turned him over to the campus police, who did no more than check out his gun and say the weapon had not been fired. The next day, Norman was observed wandering freely around the campus after it had been closed and all students, other than the "internationals," who had nowhere to go, had been sent home. He was there with the guardsmen, a so-called student. Why?

There are many more questions concerning Terry Norman's activities. Was his gun fired? If so, when and why? What has happened to his .38 revolver? Where did he get it? Was it unofficially issued to him by an official agency? Schwartzmiller, chief of the campus police at the time, categorically denied that Norman was working for his department "that day," the implication being that Norman had indeed worked for the university police on other days. Obviously, if Norman was working for the FBI on May 4, 1970, the Ohio National Guard would not be able to use him as an excuse for the misconduct of its men. This might explain why he was ignored by Ohio authorities, both military and civil. Had he been working for the campus police, on the other hand, it seems unlikely that the Guard would have overlooked his activities. Furthermore, in view of the Ohio grand jury's scathing condemnation of the campus police, it is unlikely that the special prosecutors would not have subpoenaed him to testify. They did not, however, and we have no explanation why.

Guardsman Delaney was convinced that there was more to the Norman incident than either the Justice Department or the Scranton

Commission would have us believe, and he contacted Robert Balyeat, chief prosecutor to the grand jury, and offered to testify about Norman and his gun. Initially, Balyeat expressed considerable interest and assured Delaney that the state would subpoena Norman and welcome Delaney's testimony. Time passed, and when Delaney again got in touch with the prosecutor, he was brushed off. The matter had been checked into, he was told, and there was nothing important about Norman, his conduct, or his gun.

Several other developments followed the release of *Appeal for Justice*. Arthur Krause received an anonymous letter from Akron, Ohio, which claimed that a "participating member of the Ohio National Guard the day of the Kent State massacre, May 4, 1970, was institutionalized a number of times following this incident." We had no way of uncovering the source of this information or determining its accuracy, until I received a letter from the same writer two weeks later, with the additional information that the guardsman had been divorced by his wife since the shootings. From this second letter we were able to identify the guardsman. According to the Ohio National Guard roster, he was the only noncommissioned member of Company H who had been activated for duty on May 4, 1970. Why just one enlisted man from Company H was activated is unclear, but the presence of an officer from that company at the Pagoda at the time of the shooting is of some significance. There were persistent rumors after the murders that some members of the Ohio National Guard who had not been officially activated for duty nevertheless went onto the campus in uniform. Both anonymous letters charged that a guardsman, officially listed after the fact as having been activated, but not involved in the Guard's dispersal of the noon rally, was "institutionalized" following the "Kent State massacre." It is difficult to understand the connection between his being institutionalized, if in fact he was, and the killings, just as it is hard to evaluate the significance of the alleged divorce. The anonymous writer was, apparently, attempting to alert Arthur Krause and me to an aspect of the shootings which the Justice Department had ignored: the rumors about the illegal presence of several guardsmen.

No official agency has attempted to track down these rumors, nor has it been possible to get an explanation for the presence at the Pagoda of another member of Company H—Lieutenant Ralph G. Tucker. The Justice Department, the Scranton Commission, and even Michener in his detailed account of the number of men involved and their specific units overlooked the presence of Tucker, a member of a unit that was not on the hill that day, according to official reports. The Ohio National Guard roster, as already noted, however, lists First Lieutenant Tucker as present on Blanket Hill at the time of the shooting, and states that he did not fire his weapon.

James Michener lists the guardsmen and their units who were on the football field just before the shooting:

> There were 75 Guards present, comprised as follows: two senior officers (Canterbury and Fassinger), with 53 men from Alpha Company, including three officers plus the two casuals from Charlie Company (Love and Lutey), to which were added 18 men from Troop G, including two officers. However, Major Jones now ran across the grass to join the group.

This is the group that marched from the field to the Pagoda. The official Guard roster shows Alpha Company comprised fifty-one men and three officers, making a total of fifty-four—not, as Michener has it, fifty men and three officers, or a total of fifty-three. The Justice Department summary of the FBI report says "the 96 men of Companies A and C, 145th Infantry and of Troop G, 107th Armored Cavalry were ordered to advance" at the time the entire Guard force moved out from their line near the ruins of the ROTC building. This does not include officers. The Guard roster shows that ninety-seven men were ordered to advance, and were accompanied by nine officers. Michener reported that "103 Guardsmen plus 10 officers stepped off into the history of contemporary America." The Scranton Commission was extremely vague about the number of officers and men involved, with the exception of Troop G. The Commission reported that Alpha Company comprised "some 40 to 50 men" and that Charlie Company consisted of "about 35 to 45 men." As for the number of men present on the hill at the time of the shooting, the Justice Department reports that there were fifty-three officers and men in Company A; eighteen in Troop G; and two from Company C, or a total of seventy-three. The senior officers Canterbury, Fassinger, and Jones make the total of seventy-six reported by Michener. All, however, ignore the presence of Lieutenant Tucker from Company H—which, incidentally, was a unit of the 107th Armored Cavalry—and the fact that there were fifty-four officers and men in Company A. These discrepancies indicate the less than precise manner in which this case has been handled and underscores the need for a thorough, professional investigation.

As for the total number of guardsmen, including officers, on active duty that day, the Guard rosters show that there were 722 in all, which may explain why Major Simons told CBS-TV News that Canterbury should have waited until more of the men could be assembled to support the three units hastily thrown together to disperse the assembly on the Commons. Had the general waited, Simons said, "I think we could have done a better job, without—I think we could have done the job without bloodshed." He was considerably more blunt about it off-camera, as Eszterhas and Roberts report in their book: " 'Those silly asses from Columbus,' he [Simons] was to say later. 'What are Canterbury and Del Corso doing throwing rocks? Canterbury is a general, yeah, but he is no more general material than I am.' "

Quite apart from Michael Delaney's coming forth, reaction to John Mitchell's announced decision to take no further action in the Kent State case proved to be greater than we had anticipated. In Washington, Senator Edward Kennedy, speaking at the National Press Club in late August, told newsmen that he would try to get his Senate Judiciary Subcommittee on Administrative Practice and Procedure to investigate the handling of the Kent State case by the Civil Rights Division of the Department of Justice. "Why is it we can get a federal grand jury to prosecute Daniel Ellsberg in a matter of hours," he asked, "yet this case is buried while Congress is out of town?" In New Orleans, the 250-member general board of the National Council of Churches approved, by an overwhelming majority, a resolution calling upon the Attorney General "to reconsider his decision and call a federal grand jury to afford those wronged a suitable forum for weighing the charges of conspiracy and murder brought against Ohio guardsmen and authorities." At a news conference after the passage of the resolution, Bishop John H. Burt, of the Ohio Episcopal Diocese, said the N.C.C. action was prompted by Mitchell's statement that the government was powerless to uphold the law. Kent State student Dean Kahler, paralyzed for life by a National Guard bullet, was at the news conference. He was asked by reporters if he thought Kent State had been forgotten by the American public. As a local newspaper reported: "The youth's unhesitating answer was, 'No, but I think most people are trying to forget it.' "

On the campus of Kent State University itself, two young men reacted to the Mitchell announcement by initiating a petition to President Nixon which asked simply that the Attorney General's decision be reversed so that the public debate raging around who was responsible for the four deaths on the campus "can be resolved in the dignity of our federal court system." Paul Keane, a graduate student, and Greg Rambo, then president of the Kent State Young Republicans, were deeply disturbed by Mitchell's inaction. As the two were contemplating the best course of action to take, a U.C.L.A. student, Bill Gordon, reacted to the news from Washington by writing a letter to Ken Clawson of the Washington *Post,* and it was Clawson's reply which revealed that the Nixon Administration had decided in March 1971 not to convene a federal grand jury. In his letter Clawson told Gordon that Jerris Leonard "was to have announced the Kent State decision as his last act before leaving the Civil Rights Division and assuming the post of administrator of the Law Enforcement Assistance Administration." The timing of Leonard's promotion, Clawson goes on to say—"i.e., colleges were still in session; springtime frolics resulting from making the decision public were thought probable, etc."—precluded public disclosure of the decision "until Dog Days." It was the next paragraph of this letter, however, which raised intriguing questions about the circumstances under which John Adams and I came to prepare and submit the *Appeal for Justice*.

Attorney General Mitchell had pointedly ignored Section 242 of the U.S. Code, the federal law which in terms of punishment is not as severe as the conspiracy law, Section 241. During the Kleindienst-Adams-Sindell meeting in May, the possibility of a conspiracy was raised for the first time and, to our surprise, as I have noted, was almost encouraged rather than challenged. Clawson, in his letter to Bill Gordon, said: "One of the things that helped the Justice Department in raising as few waves as Mitchell's announcement of the decision was that incredibly bad conspiracy study by—I forget the guy's name, I believe he was a New Yorker." This was, for us, the first indication that Deputy Attorney General Kleindienst might deliberately have led us into providing the Administration with a satisfactory vehicle for circumventing the law: conspiracy. After all, "no credible evidence of a conspiracy" is a more convincing excuse for inaction, especially in a case involving a United States military uniform. If Kleindienst had been honest with John Adams and said that the Civil Rights Division had already made its recommendation to the Attorney General, the *Appeal for Justice* would never have been written.

In early October 1971, Keane and Rambo worked diligently on their petition to President Nixon and in just twelve days they had collected more than ten thousand signatures. Such an outpouring of concern moved Kent State's new president, Dr. Glenn A. Olds, to agree formally to receive the petition and accompany Keane and Rambo to the White House, where the three would meet with Presidential aide Leonard Garment. Although Dr. Olds, a former U.S. delegate to the United Nations Economic and Social Council and a prominent supporter of Richard Nixon's election campaign in 1968, had declined to sign the petition on the grounds that he was not sufficiently informed about the events of May 1970, his decision to recognize that the petition represented the majority will of his university's student body was encouraging.

On Friday, October 14, in a quiet ceremony on the Commons, Dr. Olds accepted the petition, saying, "I salute, respect and honor this document." Paul Keane read a telegram sent to the students of Kent State by Senator George McGovern. "Someone must answer for Kent State," the South Dakotan said, "not with rhetoric, but with justice. Someone must answer for Kent State now, before it is written in the history books that the bloodshed here sparked the downfall of the American Republic. I call upon President Nixon to answer your plea; I urge him, as I have in the past, to convene a federal grand jury to carry out a full and open investigation of the events of May 1970. It will not bring back to life those who were slain, but it may help heal the wounds of America which were opened by the killings."

Although Mitchell's decision terminated our efforts as far as the Justice Department was concerned, the Keane-Rambo petition kept them alive to the extent that a national student petition was initiated by the Law Students Council in New York. More than forty thousand signatures were gathered in support of the ten thousand Kent State petitioners for a federal grand jury. Within the United Methodist Church, John Adams was supported by everyone involved in the Kent State issue and in particular the Board's Secretary, Dr. Dudley Ward. In New York, Carolyn D. Wilhelm, of the Board of Missions, Women's Division, got a clear sounding on the prospects that Ohio would implement its own laws. Ms. Wilhelm had written to Ohio Representative Richard Celeste in August 1971, and in his reply of October 27 he said, quite frankly: "There is no glimmer of interest in reopening the inquiry into the Kent shootings." He told Ms. Wilhelm that he had discussed the matter with Jim Friedman, Governor Gilligan's executive counsel, and from their conversation learned that the liberal Democrat did not share Senator McGovern's view that "someone must answer for Kent State now." As for the House of Representatives in Ohio, Celeste said, "Shocking as it may seem, the general consensus is that any further inquiry will only lead to more repressive actions toward the students and rekindle tensions on the campus. . . . No one felt that a state investigation would adequately explore the responsibility of the National Guard, or certain of its members, for the shootings." In conclusion, he noted that "a handful of legislators are quite interested in assisting further inquiry into what really happened at Kent," including himself, but they were "in no position to initiate such an inquiry."

November 12, 1971, marked the publication of Ron Henderson's impressive special supplement issue of *American Report,* a review, sponsored by Clergy and Laymen Concerned, of the Justice Department's failure to uphold federal law and of the reaction over a period of eighteen months to the murders at Kent State. The executive director of the Joint Washington Office for Social Concern, Robert E. Jones, contributed a penetrating analysis of the Nixon Administration as "anti-student." Jones, a key figure in the Washington Interreligious Staff Council, charged that in a "whole series of actions and non-actions the Administration has demonstrated this anti-student bent." He noted that in "both the 1968 and 1970 campaigns, the specter of campus violence and radicalism was used to frighten the voters. Hardhats have been played up by the President and his Administration; witness the invitation to construction workers' leaders to visit the White House shortly after students and hardhats mixed it up in counter-demonstrations on the Cambodia war issue." Addressing himself to Mitchell's decision not to convene a federal grand jury, Jones called it "a singular non-action" and "the latest manifestation of Administration attitudes toward the student population." Federal grand juries, he observed, "have been convened on far less substance."

Another contributor to *American Report*'s supplement was Professor Jerry M. Lewis of Kent State University, who pointed out that if the guardsmen who wheeled around in unison and started shooting had not done so on a concerted decision, the law of averages would have had at least one of them turning in the opposite direction from the rest. Since they had fixed bayonets on their rifles, anyone turning the wrong way to the others might well have injured the man next to him. Yet the guardsmen claim they fired in self-defense, on the basis of individual decisions as to the degree of danger to their lives, precisely at the same split second.

The most extensive report in the supplement is devoted to Ron Henderson's interviews with Arthur Krause, Florence Schroeder, and Martin and Sarah Scheuer. It is a penetrating portrait of parental anguish. "No major tragedy had ever hit our family," Mrs. Schroeder said. "When it did we thought, well, things turn out for other people, so things will turn out all right for us. When we heard that Mr. Krause was doubting—he was using the word 'whitewash'—we didn't quite believe it and it took us a little bit longer to get into, not a battle, but it is a search. The church is now using the term 'appeal for justice,' and that's where we're going to stay until it comes."

Arthur Krause recalled the Orangeburg killings of 1968 and the bombing of three black children in Birmingham and his failure to respond to those murders. "I feel a great sense of guilt because I realized what was going on but I didn't do a damn thing about it." Like most Americans these days, he said, we sit on the fence and "depend on the lawyer, the church, and the government" to do whatever should be done, "but if the government doesn't have the right people in the job nothing will be done, and we must have good government and we, the people, have to make the government good. Apathy will not be part of my makeup anymore. Apathy is what caused Kent State."

Martin Scheuer, echoing the sentiments of so many immigrants to this country, said he always had great confidence in American justice. "I was born in Europe and I always looked up to America as a place where there was more justice than any other country in the world. And with a few exceptions I always expected equal justice for everybody in America." The brutal shooting down of his daughter Sandy shattered that confidence and ultimately undermined his faith in American judicial equity. "Lately I think we have too much corruption in the upper levels of the government," he went on, "and justice can be bought out. And now we have a lot of injustices—not only in our case but in other cases too."

Mrs. Sarah Scheuer, responding to a question about public reaction to the murders, touched upon the heart of the problem: "I think that for a lot of people in America, when the kids were shot at Kent, it was the same as getting revenge for the bombing in Wisconsin, or damage that was done any place where there have been bombings by any students. They were shooting the Weathermen, they were shooting members of SDS; our four were symbolic—or the 13, let's put it that way—were symbolic of all the destruction that had come about. They think now that because of these shootings it has stopped everything and that justifies the killing in their mind. 'Well, we've killed four but look at all that we've saved since then.' "

On November 16, 1971, the Ohio Council of Churches called on President Nixon to convene a federal grand jury to investigate the Kent State shootings. At the Council's fifty-third annual assembly, the resolution was adopted, with a few delegates dissenting. Bishop Burt told the Akron *Beacon Journal* that he hoped the resolution would inspire "a groundswell of public opinion calling for justice to be done." The Council had also voted in favor of an appeal both to the U.S. Attorney General and to Ohio's attorney general for a review of existing laws, to determine where, if at all, they fail to protect citizens "from unwarranted use of force by persons acting under color of law." Bishop Burt stressed the fact that the Council's resolution did not imply guilt or responsibility on the part of anyone involved in Kent State. "We didn't take sides," he said. "We simply said, 'let justice be done.' "

These resolutions, like the students' petition and individual appeals, fell on deaf ears in Washington. The President's aide, Leonard Garment, was keeping Rambo and Keane at bay with promises of serious consideration of their petition and an early answer. He even said it would be helpful, in reviewing Mitchell's decision, to have a brief stating the key unanswered questions. Such a brief was immediately prepared and sent to Garment. In December, it was learned that the petition, along with petitions from other colleges across the country, had been sent to the Justice Department. Mr. Mitchell was to review the appeal for a reversal of Mr. Mitchell's decision.

At least one man was listening, however: James Michener. Michener had read our *Appeal for Justice,* and in December 1971 he wrote to John Adams expressing his approval of the work we were doing in behalf of the families of the Kent State victims. It was in this letter that Michener reinforced the somewhat obscure suggestion in his book that some kind of decision had been reached on the practice field to shoot at the students. "I think the only substantive difference that might exist between us," he said, "is the time definition of the word conspiracy. I have told everyone who has queried me on the matter that if you are legally right, that conspiracy could consist of merely a few moments, then your case is irrefutable." He went on to say that he "found no fault in either the methodology or the conclusions you reached" in the *Appeal*.

In the conclusion to the *Appeal for Justice,* I had written: "The killing of four students at Kent State now stands as a classic example of justice delayed, circumvented and mocked. Very few tragedies like this are so extensively photographed, and very few occur in conditions where so many witnesses are able to provide investigators with so much invaluable information. Unlike the inexcusable shootings at South Carolina State in 1968 and Jackson State in 1970, the killings at Kent State took place in broad daylight beneath a brilliant sun. Consequently we have an almost step-by-step record of what happened on May 4, 1970, and this record suggests that the shooting began as the result of a planned and pre-arranged act involving a certain number of guardsmen."

The New Year of 1972 offered us about as much hope for justice as had the New Year of 1971. Much was being written, but nothing was happening. James Ahern's book, *Police in Trouble,* came out in 1972, and the former member of President Nixon's Commission on Campus Unrest did not mince words. "There is a wealth of evidence concerning the Kent State and Jackson State killings that has not been released to the public," he wrote. "The FBI has eight thousand pages on Kent State alone. And a news leak in the Akron *Beacon Journal* indicated some time ago that—although the FBI emphatically denies ever evaluating evidence—certain members of the Bureau felt confident concerning a possibility of successful prosecution at least in the Kent State case." About the Justice Department's decision to do nothing, Ahern said: "Behavior of this kind on the part of the highest prosecutorial agency in the country threatens to confirm the most radical criticisms of the American system of justice that have been brought against it in recent years." And he added: "The political motivation in the Justice Department's refusal to prosecute at least the Kent State case seems blatant, crass and cynical."

One encouraging political development came early in 1972 when Republican Senator Robert Taft, Jr., of Ohio, a stanch opponent of a federal grand jury investigation, expressed interest in the implementation of a Congressional inquiry into May 4, 1970. In correspondence with the student-petition organizers, Keane and Rambo, Taft stated that he had written to Senator Edward Kennedy proposing a meeting between the two to explore the possibilities of Kennedy's Senate Judiciary Subcommittee conducting a probe. By July of 1972 Taft was so convinced of the need for an investigation outside the Justice

Department that he informed the press that Kennedy's subcommittee "will open hearings soon into the Kent State University killings of four students." However, in a press conference reported in the Lorain *Journal*, Bill Schroeder's home-town newspaper, Senator Taft conceded that "any hearings before the November elections are doubtful because they might be influenced by the political atmosphere."

On the second anniversary of the Kent State killings, some of the families agreed to go to Washington to place black wreaths at the doors of the White House and the Justice Department. John Adams coordinated the plans and obtained the necessary government permits, even providing the assurance that after the demonstration the wreaths would be removed by the demonstrators.

On May 2, however, news came of the death of J. Edgar Hoover, and the funeral was announced for noon on May 4, the very time when we were to place the wreaths. In deference to the national loss and out of respect for Mr. Hoover and his service to his country, the families canceled their journey to Washington.

In connection with their planned journey to Washington, the families of the four killed, along with those of Dean Kahler, Joseph Lewis, Thomas Grace, Douglas Wrentmore, and Donald MacKenzie, had written to President Nixon, asking for an opportunity to meet with the President or the Attorney General. The letter was transmitted to the White House by Dr. Dean Kelley of the National Council of Churches, on April 29, 1972. There was no reply.

On May 24 I wrote once more to President Nixon. I recalled the eulogy recently delivered at the funeral of J. Edgar Hoover and in particular the President's lofty words that the nation wants to return to respect for law. "We do indeed want respect for law," I said, "but your government has so far pointedly refused to live up to your exhortation of May 4th this year when it comes to the injustice of Kent State." I concluded: "For the dead at Kent State, for the maimed, for the wounded, for the student petitioners, and for these parents, I beg you do not say we want to return to respect for law until you are ready and willing to lead us by example of what respect for the law really means."

To my surprise, I received a reply from Leonard Garment two weeks later. In it Garment said, like a record with a stuck needle, that the "substance of issues which you and the parents have raised is still under consideration at the Department of Justice." He could say this, despite the fact that Attorney General-designate Kleindienst had told the Senate Judiciary Committee earlier in the year that the Kent State file was closed and that the Department was not reviewing its decision. Garment also expressed the hope that I would inform the parents of the President's decision not to meet with them. The White House would not even answer those mothers and fathers but asked me to do it for them. I wrote back to say I could not contain my shock at his office's effrontery. A month later I received a bulging envelope from the White House, containing copies of nine two-page letters from Garment, one for each of the families who had written to the President. The letters were identical.

Your letter of April 19, sent through the National Council of Churches, reached us on May 1. Mr. Krause had discussed the letter with me after it arrived, and a more formal acknowledgment was sent to Mr. Davies on June 6.

The new Attorney General was asked about this matter in a public question and answer session and has answered for himself and for the Administration that he has not seen presented to him sufficient new evidence or information which would compel him to reverse the decision of former Attorney General Mitchell concerning the submittal of this matter to a Federal Grand Jury.

Willfulness or specific criminal intent or planned or purposeful conspiracy must be proved in order to support a federal indictment; there is still no evidence available to prove such a violation of the Federal criminal statutes.

Garment's letter called to mind the Orangeburg incident, in the aftermath of which the Justice Department exercised the full powers at its command in cases involving the use of lethal force by law-enforcement officers. On the night of February 8, 1968, state highway police opened fire on the campus of South Carolina State College at Orangeburg, killing three and wounding twenty-seven students who were protesting against a segregated bowling alley and alleged police brutality. Seven months later, assistant Attorney General Stephen Pollak, at that time head of the Civil Rights Division, recommended to Attorney General Ramsey Clark that the Justice Department convene a federal grand jury to investigate the circumstances surrounding the fatal shootings. Although nine patrolmen had admitted to FBI agents they had fired into the crowd—just as five Ohio National Guardsmen so admitted to the FBI in the Kent State case—Pollak recommended that the government go before the grand jury not to seek indictments but rather to get testimony on record and see what evidence might be uncovered that would warrant asking for indictments in the course of the grand-jury hearings. Jack Nelson and Jack Bass, authors of the book *The Orangeburg Massacre,* report that Pollak opted for this approach because "there were unanswered questions and conflicting evidence" which the head of the Civil Rights Division "felt might be resolved by testimony before the jury." Attorney General Clark and Stephen Pollak, according to Nelson and Bass, believed "that the probabilities of a conviction should not be a criterion for determining whether to prosecute as long as the government believed a crime had been committed and the perpetrators had been identified." Obviously the Nixon Administration does not share this belief when it comes to Kent State, but it has made it clear that it does subscribe to Clark's philosophy when it comes to Leslie Bacon, Philip Berrigan, and Daniel Ellsberg.

Testimony at the grand-jury hearings in South Carolina did, in fact, produce sufficient evidence for the government to seek indictments. The federal grand jury declined, but the evidence was such that on December 19, 1968, Pollak recommended implementation of still another tool available to the Justice Department. He recommended to Ramsey Clark that the Justice Department file "a criminal information" against the nine patrolmen who had admitted firing into the crowd, and thereby bring them to trial even though the federal grand jury had not returned any indictments. Pollak's recommendation was approved.

Because the U.S. attorney in Columbia, South Carolina, had refused to take part in the Justice Department's action, the criminal-information papers were signed by Robert Hocutt, at that time an attorney in the Civil Rights Division. Pollak was well aware of the difficulties facing the government's pursuit of justice. But he "felt the [Justice] Department had a responsibility to present the case and he believed that a trial in open court—regardless of the verdict—would have a deterrent effect on police misconduct." If the government "only brought cases in which you get a jury conviction," he told Nelson and Bass, "you would bring very few cases . . . Laws are enacted to protect people from having police taking the law into their own hands."

The charge in the Orangeburg case alleged that the nine patrolmen, "acting under color of the laws of the State of South Carolina, did wilfully discharge and shoot firearms into a group of persons on the campus of South Carolina State College . . . thereby killing, injuring and intimidating persons in said group, with the intent of imposing summary punishment upon those persons, and did thereby deprive those persons of the right, secured and protected by the Constitution of the United States, not to be deprived of life or liberty without due process of law."

The government's case against the South Carolina patrolmen was keyed to the number of times six of the nine defendants had fired their weapons. Charles Quaintance, prosecuting, "argued that repeated shooting was an offensive act, rather than a defensive one, and declared that to acquit all the defendants 'would be to say when the going gets rough, the enforcers of the law are permitted to act beyond the law; and that those who are sworn to uphold the law may disregard the law.' "

While Orangeburg stands as an example of federal officials enforcing the laws they were sworn to uphold, even though there were no indictments or convictions, Kent State stands as an example of abuse of those laws by an administration more receptive to political-popularity polls than to the interests of justice.

Leonard Garment's letter to the families went on to note the civil litigation under way in Ohio, which is "quite another matter and will have to be left up to the courts of the State of Ohio." He added:

> There is not an official in this entire Administration, from the President and the Attorney General on down, who is indifferent to your own personal grief at the death and injury which occurred on that day in May two years ago. As John Mitchell said, the President's Commission was right in terming the rifle fire as "unnecessary, unwarranted and inexcusable." But there is still no evidence known to the Attorney General of a federally punishable conspiracy.

A meeting with President Nixon or Kleindienst, the letter concluded—"however much either of them would like to do so to demonstrate his personal compassion for your own sorrow"—would not in any way change the "basic facts." And the last sentence reiterated once more the Administration's familiar position on Kent State, the pious wish that no more students will be killed by trigger-happy National Guardsmen. "We can hope that the nation will pay attention to the lessons of this tragedy and that nothing like it will ever happen again."

Perhaps the most insensitive aspect of Leonard Garment's letter was his sending copies to Dr. Glenn Olds, Paul Keane, and Greg Rambo, who had not participated in this exchange of correspondence. This, then, was the Nixon Administration's formal response to the fifty thousand citizens who had signed the petition for a federal grand jury. On July 13, 1972, Keane and Rambo asked Garment's aide, Brad Patterson, if the letter represented the Administration's rejection of the petition. The government's response to the petition, Patterson said, had in fact been given by Kleindienst in his first press conference after being confirmed as Attorney General. That was on June 13, 1972, but Keane and Rambo had not been accorded the courtesy of a notification to that effect. During the news conference, Kleindienst had been asked whether the question of convening a federal grand jury on Kent State had ever been resolved. The new Attorney General noted that he had been on several campuses throughout the country and had been asked this question by students. "I've said publicly and I've said before the Senate Judiciary Committee that there has not been presented to me, since I have been the Acting Attorney General, sufficient new evidence or information or material that would compel me to reverse the decision of Mr. Mitchell concerning the submittal of this matter to a Federal grand jury."

"I don't want to appear insensitive or callous," Kleindienst added. "I think you all know about my family and the affinity I have toward young people, but I don't know to what extent the Attorney General of the United States, in the proper execution of his responsibilities, is called upon to respond to matters of this kind that don't come about in the ordinary operation of our Department."

The Garment letter elicited a response from Professor David Engdahl of the Law Revision Center at the University of Colorado. He concedes that the evidence publicly available of a possible conspiracy to shoot at the students is only circumstantial, "but it is strong." An Administration that is "intent upon justice would invoke the statute recently upheld by the Supreme Court granting some of the guardsmen immunity for their testimony before a grand jury to secure more direct evidence to either confirm or dispel the suspicions of conspiracy which the circumstances reasonably induce." Professor Engdahl also points out that "even those few facts of the Kent shootings that have escaped the net of secrecy and come to public attention, leave no room for doubting" the Justice Department's own summary of the FBI report, which, he noted, is "now discreetly sequestered in the National Archives." It "need not be proved that the guardsmen were conscious of the 'chapter and verse' of the Constitution when they acted," Engdahl goes on. "It need only be proved that they specifically intended to deprive persons of some right or privilege, which happens to be a right or privilege that is constitutionally secured." Engdahl also says: "From these facts and others already public, not to mention the additional facts concealed by the Administration in the Archives and the further facts that a conscientious prosecutorial effort could disclose, it might very well appear beyond a reasonable doubt that the requisite specific intent was present. Without question, there is at least far more than adequate evidence to support a grand jury's indictment on probable cause."

Taking note of Garment's assurance that the entire Administration felt deeply sorry for the parents of the dead, Engdahl added: "Do not deceive yourself into believing that words of sympathy and the recitation of legal formulas can answer the call of these parents for justice. It is not the law that denies them the justice they seek. It is transparently the prosecutorial discretion of this Administration. Let the onus rest where it belongs. The law is adequate were it enforced."

As for the pious wish that nothing like Kent State would ever happen again and that the nation has learned the lessons of the killings, the Colorado law professor asked Garment what those lessons were. "That our children must not misbehave on campus lest they be shot in the back by angry soldiers dispatched by the government whose policies they protest? That lesson has been learned, and the campuses are, for now at least, relatively quiet, if not really at peace. But there are other lessons: There is the lesson of Allison—that disrespect is a capital crime. And the lesson of Sandy—that innocent passers-by are also fair targets. And the lesson of Bill Schroeder—that even a straight ROTC cadet had better not turn his back on his brothers-in-arms maintaining the peace with their weapons of war. And the lessons which this Administration has made perfectly clear—that justice can be put off with a simple, 'Gee, I'm sorry.' " Finally, there is an old lesson that monarchs and governments throughout history have failed to learn until too late: that "free men—until they lose their resolve to be free—will not long endure their government's willingness to suppress even riots, not to mention lesser disorders, with the indiscriminate vengeance of military force."

On July 27, 1972, Leonard Garment officially confirmed the President's decision to reject the student petition. Garment's letter to Keane and Rambo consists of one paragraph:

> This is a personal note of apology for my failure to write to the two of you when I wrote to the parents. There is not much I could have added, certainly nothing of substance, but it was the least I could have done in view of our meetings and dealings and the sincerity of purpose and good faith with which you conducted yourselves throughout.

After ten months of effort, that was it. Paul Keane promptly wrote to Dr. Olds: "I am sure that you will be heartened to know that after ten months of spending enormous amounts of energy and money on a petition drive designed to reaffirm students' faith in the 'System,' by invoking the noble machinery of American justice, all we have to show for it is this lousy paragraph from your friend, Leonard Garment." He concluded his letter by asking the Kent State University president, "What are we supposed to do with it? Reproduce it for all incoming freshmen with the hopeful assertion: You, too, may one day know the exhilaration of participating in the American 'System.' "

On August 3, Senator Robert Taft, Jr., of Ohio, responded to a letter from Arthur Krause. The senator expressed his belief that a federal grand-jury investigation would be "a frustrating experience for all concerned" and not likely "to result in indictments." However, "a further hearing on the matter might resolve unanswered questions and show that under our system there is a forum offering such a remedy." On the same day, in a letter to Keane and Rambo, Senator Taft wrote, "I appreciate your support for my efforts for a Congressional Committee to convene on the subject of the Kent State tragedy. The Subcommittee which I believe to be the most appropriate for this task is the Subcommittee on Administrative Practice and Procedure, chaired by Senator Kennedy."

A week later, Paul Keane and Greg Rambo joined with Bill Gordon and Robert Gage, president of the Kent State student body, in letters to the chairmen of the Senate and House Judiciary Committees, asking for a Congressional investigation into "why the Justice Department refuses to convene a Federal grand jury to investigate the shootings on our campus in May, 1970." The four said they were "tired of getting the run-around and being lied to" and wanted Congress to "get the answers which the White House and Justice Department refuse to give us." A report, prepared by Bill Gordon, detailing the Keane-Rambo efforts, was sent along with the letters to Senator Eastland and Congressman Celler. It was also sent to other members of Congress, including Senator Kennedy, who had been trying to get answers out of the Justice Department for almost a year. On August 17, 1972, Kennedy wrote to Attorney General Kleindienst, forwarding a copy of Gordon's history of the student petition. "It is extremely unfortunate," Senator Kennedy wrote, "to have added to the tragedy of the Kent State killings themselves the additional element of a course of federal dealings which leaves tens of thousands of Americans with a feeling that they are being deceived by their government."

Kennedy acknowledged that "many of the issues of good faith and veracity raised" in the report are secondary to the essential point of the May 4 shootings, which is "to satisfy the people of Kent State, the parents of the victims, and all Americans that the Executive Branch of the Federal government exhausted all the resources and powers at its disposal to discover, obtain evidence of, and prosecute any possible federal crimes committed in the course of what was truly a national disaster of historic proportions." Kennedy again asked for Kleindienst's cooperation in serving the interests of justice by making available to his subcommittee "the materials on which the Department of Justice based its decision not to convene a Grand Jury (with its resultant inability to utilize subpoenas, immunity grants and other investigative procedures used regularly in contemporaneous cases) or otherwise to proceed against any of those involved in the shootings."

On September 5, 1972, the organizers of the student petition wrote once more to Leonard Garment: "Kindly return immediately the 50,000 signatures received by your office for the petition asking President Nixon to convene a Federal Grand Jury investigation of the Kent State murders." This request was promptly complied with, and the petitions now rest at Kent State University.

On September 17, 1972, the Akron *Beacon Journal* reported that four attorneys representing Ohio National Guardsmen had asked the state of Ohio—that is, the taxpayers of Ohio—to pay them a total of $77,065 in fees.

The claims were filed with Ohio's Sundry Claims Board, which approved the claims on September 26, and so the taxpayers of Ohio have footed the bill for legal work on behalf of the guardsmen which it is extremely difficult to define, inasmuch as no guardsman, except for Generals Canterbury and Del Corso and Captain Raymond Srp, has been deeply involved in the civil litigation initiated by the families of the dead and wounded at Kent State. For the parents, of course, the financial obligation has become enormous, and were it not for committed people such as attorney Steven Sindell and Professor Engdahl, much of the legal work could not have been done. It was for these lawyers that the Fund to Secure Due Process of Law in the Kent State murders was established by the National Council of Churches.

On October 12, 1972, I joined with some Kent State families and victims in a *mandamus* action to compel Attorney General Kleindienst to cease standing in the way of a federal grand jury investigation. The parents of the dead, along with Dean Kahler and Joseph Lewis, were supported in the action by Joseph Rhodes, Jr., and John Adams in the capacity of individual citizen. This lawsuit, filed in the United States District Court for the District of Columbia, charged that the decision made by John Mitchell, affirmed by the present Attorney General, Richard Kleindienst, "precluding even a presentation of the evidence already assembled to a federal grand jury for its further investigation," was "a willful, arbitrary, capricious, bad-faith, discriminatory, and lawless abuse of discretion, wholly inconsistent with constitutional and statutory duties to see that the laws are faithfully executed, and said decision was beyond the limits of permissible and legitimate prosecutorial discretion, being based upon considerations inappropriate to prosecutorial discretion, thereby in excess of the lawful exercise of his jurisdiction." The complaint concluded: "All avenues have been exhausted in appealing to the Executive Branch for a federal grand jury investigation. Such efforts include petitions containing tens of thousands of signatures presented to the President of the United States, and numerous requests made to the Justice Department—all to no avail. Plaintiffs now come before this court having no further relief known to them." Our attorneys in this final legal effort to force the Nixon Administration to uphold the law— Steven Sindell, David Engdahl, and Louis J. Morse of Washington, D.C.—were acting again out of commitment to the issue of Kent State and what it symbolizes for the future.

In describing the action taken against Kleindienst, Professor Engdahl said there had never before been "such sharp and calculated charges leveled against an Attorney General of the United States in legal proceedings." He went on to admit: one "can only speculate as to the motive that might explain the apparently deliberate effort to bury the Kent State matter." It is, he said, quite possible "that the Administration does have something to hide." If not, then "perhaps the President's too-candid admission that he regards dissenting students as 'bums' reflects a prejudice so profound that he simply does not perceive the issues posed by Kent State."

At the time the *mandamus* action was filed, Arthur Krause appealed to the Supreme Court of the United States for the right to a day in court in behalf of his dead daughter. This action, begun in 1970, alleged that the state of Ohio bore responsibility for the criminally negligent conduct of its agents which caused the death of his child. Initially the suit was dismissed, but on appeal Krause was upheld in a two-to-one decision which repudiated Ohio's sovereign-immunity concept of law. The state appealed to Ohio's Supreme Court and, not surprisingly, won out, thereby forcing Krause to plead in vain before the highest court in the nation. In that appeal, Attorneys Steven and Joseph M. Sindell said:

> It is striking that such considerable protection is afforded the rights of the lowliest accused, even a drunk driver, and yet your appellant herein, Arthur Krause, must yet convince this court to afford civil redress to protect not the accused, but the victim. Surely the innocent victims of this society, the Allison Krauses and their parents, are entitled to the same consideration in the prosecution of their civil rights—including the necessity to make their rights effective—as the defendant accused of committing a misdemeanor. This is not just a matter of legislation; it is a matter of fundamental constitutional justice.

There is no escaping the fact that it is not so much the laws that are inadequate as the men who administer them. Men who can piously proclaim their respect for human life and its preciousness, and expound about their Justice Department's being second to none in its concern for constitutional rights and how they are leading us back to respect for the law. But the shallowness of their rhetoric is painfully apparent. Kent State, as *The Christian Science Monitor* said, is going to haunt the Nixon Administration for a long time to come, because the lessons of those deaths have been ignored by the government. The dead at Kent State ceased long ago to be victims. The Nixon Administration has transformed their deaths into a nagging and persistent challenge to our conscience.

We can, of course, ignore this challenge, as many have for three years. But can we really afford to ignore the government's abrogation of its sworn obligation to our Constitution and our laws?

It was not until May 10, 1973, shortly after former Attorney General Mitchell's indictment by a New York federal grand jury on charges of perjury and obstructing justice, that Deputy Assistant Attorney General William O'Connor admitted that the Justice Department had for some time possessed evidence upon which to seek indictments against one to six Ohio guardsmen for depriving the victims of their civil rights without due process of law. O'Connor's remarks, made to Keane, Rambo, and Dean Kahler at a White House meeting, and subsequently reported by several newsmen, constituted the first time the government has conceded that prosecutable evidence existed. When pressed by David Hess of Knight Newspapers to explain why no action was taken, O'Connor said it would have been inappropriate to prosecute a few guardsmen for "misdemeanors" in a case of such "magnitude." Besides, he claimed, the evidence was "pretty thin stuff." Responding to questions by Florence Moukley and Trudy Rubin of *The Christian Science Monitor,* O'Connor said that indictments on the evidence available were not sought because "successful prosecution is unlikely." Arthur Krause reacted to O'Connor's remarks by telling *The Monitor* that "not to convene a federal grand jury when there is any possibility of indictment means that the Justice Department is acting as judge and jury."

There is, as O'Connor's statement confirms, no end to this book, because the struggle for justice in a free society never ends. If the American people had recognized from the beginning that the shooting down of unarmed civilians on a crowded college campus by combat-equipped troops was wrong, the Justice Department would have responded to the political will of the majority. Instead, the shootings were generally condoned. Whether this book will inspire you to ask the questions about Kent State that we have been asking for three years, only time will tell. But of one thing there can be no doubt: our quest for justice will continue. It will continue because we hear and understand the warning that Richard Harris sounds at the conclusion of his book *Justice.*

Perhaps the best way to judge Mitchell's stewardship of the high office he holds is by accepting his earlier suggestion: "You will be better advised to watch what we do instead of what we say." Anyone who watches with any care must be compelled to conclude that the policies of Barry Goldwater and the right wing, which the voters overwhelmingly repudiated in 1964, have become the policies of the government today. Most people no longer seem to care—if, indeed, they know—what is happening to their country. Exhausted by the demands of modern life and muddled by the fearful discord tearing at society, they seem to have turned their common fate over to their leaders in a way that would have been inconceivable five years ago, when the public rejected extremist appeals for more war in Vietnam and less justice at home. And their leaders—convinced that this abdication means agreement, and that agreement means the public interest is being served—manage the people's affairs in a way that can only divide the country further. When the people finally awaken, they may find their freedoms gone, because the abandonment of the rule of law must bring on tyranny. Since it is the majority's fear—fear of black men, fear of crime, fear of disorder, fear even of differences— that allows repression to flourish, those who succumb to their fears are as responsible as those who make political use of them. And in the end both will suffer equally. "For they have sown the wind, and they shall reap the whirlwind."

epilogue
Kent State to
Southern University

We can only hope that
any type of recurrence
can be avoided by this
experience and that in-
cidents like this will
never again be part of
our national life.

John N. Mitchell
U.S. Attorney General
August 13, 1971

With these concluding words to his statement on the closing of the Kent State file, Mitchell underscored the extent of the Nixon Administration's interest in law enforcement when the victims are college students, white or black. Fifteen months later, two male students at Southern University in Baton Rouge, Louisiana, were "accidentally" shot to death during an attempt by state police to clear student demonstrators from the university's administration building, which had been occupied to protest campus living conditions and force the resignation of Dr. G. Leon Netterville, Jr., president of Southern University. The killing of the two students, Denver A. Smith and Leonard Douglas Brown, occurred in broad daylight on November 16, 1972, and was recorded on film by television cameramen. In a very real sense these two deaths are the cruel and unnecessary consequence of this Administration's substitution of a pious wish in place of the pursuit of justice and of the deterrent effect on police misconduct that equal enforcement of the laws violated at Kent State would inevitably have generated.

In *The Orangeburg Massacre,* Jack Nelson and Jack Bass conclude their study of the 1968 killings on the campus of South Carolina State College with an appendix entitled "Orangeburg to Kent State." Nelson and Bass note the similarities between the two incidents and then get to the core of the problem: "The real tragedy is that there were lessons to be learned from the Orangeburg incident: lessons in how not to exacerbate a situation of mounting student tension and frustration and in how not to handle student demonstrations. Ohio officials learned nothing from the South Carolina experience." And now Louisiana officials have demonstrated how much they learned from the Ohio experience. This senseless wheel continues to turn, because the most important lesson of all—that a law-enforcement uniform is not a cloak of immunity from accountability before the bar of justice—is not taught by the agencies of federal and state government responsible for

206

upholding our laws. The deliberate and politically motivated abrogation of constitutional obligations encourages official misconduct and establishes a pattern that almost guarantees that incidents like Kent State and Southern University will continue to be part of our national life.

"South Carolina officials," Nelson and Bass report, "blamed the Orangeburg trouble on snipers and outside agitators. They never produced a sniper and there was overwhelming evidence that the patrolmen were not fired upon immediately before opening fire. No patrolmen were struck by gunfire." Ohio officials blamed Kent State on "snipers and outside agitators." Mississippi officials blamed Jackson State on a sniper, which they were unable to produce. "Even if there was sniper fire at Jackson State," the Scranton Commission concluded, "—a question on which we have found conflicting evidence—the 28-second barrage of lethal gunfire, partly directed into crowded windows of Alexander Hall and into a crowd in front of Alexander Hall, was completely unwarranted and unjustified." Louisiana officials blamed Southern University on the students for firing a tear-gas canister at the advancing policemen, and on outsiders. Governor Edwin Edwards told newsmen, according to *The New York Times* of November 17, 1972, that "it was entirely possible that the unidentified dead man was an 'outsider.'" Later the victim was identified as Leonard Douglas Brown, a student at the university. Al Amiss, sheriff of the East Baton Rouge Parish County, followed to the letter the pattern set by Generals Del Corso and Canterbury in Ohio: "I ordered the students to move out. There were 2,000 of them." (Governor Edwards said there were about three hundred, a figure borne out by films of the incident.) "We gave them five minutes to move out, and then we moved toward the middle of them. They did a flanking maneuver to the right of the [administration] building and, the next thing I knew, they threw tear-gas canisters and fragmentation bombs." The police responded with tear gas. "As far as I know," Sheriff Amiss told the press, "none of our men fired shotguns or their rifles." And he added: "We heard two shots from pistols from the crowd."

In all four incidents—Orangeburg, Jackson, Kent, and Baton Rouge—there is strong public evidence that the killings were committed by individuals acting independently and without authority. Nelson and Bass, in comparing Orangeburg and Kent State, noted that in "both instances a senior state official was on the scene and ostensibly in command—Chief J. P. Strom of the State Law Enforcement Division at Orangeburg and Assistant Adjutant General Robert Canterbury at Kent State—but neither had control of the situation." At Jackson State there were two commanders: Inspector Lloyd Jones in charge of forty Mississippi highway patrolmen, and Lieutenant

Warren Magee in charge of twenty-six Jackson City policemen. Major General Walter Johnson, adjutant general of the Mississippi National Guard, was present nearby but was not involved at the time of the shootings. He arrived shortly thereafter and, the Scranton Commission reports, promptly "approached Inspector Jones and asked who had issued the order to fire. Jones said, 'No one.'" Lieutenant Magee reportedly started shouting "Cease fire! Cease fire!"—just as General Canterbury and Major Jones allegedly did at Kent State—but neither the policemen at Jackson State nor the guardsmen at Kent State obeyed the orders. On the contrary, they continued firing for twenty-eight and thirteen seconds, respectively. At Southern University, only one or possibly two law officers fired into the crowd of students fleeing from in front of the administration building. The two shots that Sheriff Amiss heard were ascribed to the police after autopsy reports indicated that the two students had been hit in the head with buckshot. It would seem that in this instance there was no order to fire. But in the other three cases, too many men participated in a sustained volley and did so in too organized and coordinated a manner for it to be likely that the fusillades occurred spontaneously, without some kind of prior decision or signal. How valid these assumptions may be can only be determined in a court of law, but both in the Kent State and in the Jackson State shootings public officials have ensured that this forum is denied.

On November 20, 1972, Louisiana's Attorney General William J. Guste, Jr., duly announced the convening of a commission to investigate "the unrest that resulted in the deaths of two students at Southern University." The commission would have the authority enjoyed by a grand jury and be in a position to assemble evidence for possible criminal prosecutions "against any agency, law enforcement and others."

Ten days after the killing of Brown and Smith in Louisiana, Governor Edwards conceded that the first tear-gas canister might have been fired not by the students at the police but vice versa. One of the television films seemed to show the canister coming from the demonstrators, but another film, according to the November 28 *New York Times,* "showed a tear-gas canister fired from the ranks of the police and a student picking it up and tossing it back, setting off a barrage of tear gas by the police." This concession, however, did not hamper the governor when he testified at a public inquiry convened by black leaders under the chairmanship of Haywood Burns, director of the National Conference of Black Lawyers. "The precipitating event," Governor Edwards told the group, "was the firing of a tear-gas missile, fired from the building by students, a rifle-like shot into the midst of the deputy sheriffs." The governor's claim, the *Times* reported, "brought hisses, shouts and groans from the predominantly black audience in a black section of the city."

We have surrendered so much of our authority to our public servants that government in America today can lie, cheat, and deceive to a degree that would have been unthinkable at the time of Sherman Adams's fall from power less than two decades ago. Even the Scranton Commission was moved to make the following comment in its report on the Jackson State murders: "In the hours after the shooting and for months thereafter, the statements of some city police officers established a pattern of deceit."

Jack Nelson and Jack Bass concluded their comparison between Orangeburg and Kent State, and their book, with the following observation: "Another vital difference, of course, was that the Orangeburg victims were black. If they had been white, perhaps the nation would have learned something from 'The Orangeburg Massacre.' " The assumption was that justice would be done at Kent State because the victims were from white, middle-class American families. That assumption was wrong. The color of the victims' skin has nothing to do with how the law is enforced in the aftermath of an incident. The victims here were all students, college students, and the Nixon Administration has made perfectly clear its feelings about students.

The tragedy at Southern University shows, at the very least, that the lessons we have been urged to learn from the tragedies at Orangeburg, Kent State, and Jackson State have not been learned. The Scranton Commission said its reports on Kent and Jackson had attempted to define those lessons, "lessons that the Guard, police, students, faculty, administrators, government at all levels, and the American people must learn—and begin, at once, to act upon." When Samuel Hammond, Jr., Delano Middleton, and Henry Smith were shot to death at Orangeburg in 1968, Attorney General Ramsey Clark and the Johnson Administration sought to the limit of their powers to define the lessons to be learned through equal enforcement of the law. When Sandy Scheuer, Allison Krause, Bill Schroeder, and Jeff Miller were shot to death at Kent State in 1970, Attorney General John Mitchell and the Nixon Administration sought to circumvent their powers by misleading the American people as to the scope of those powers. Ten days later, Phillip Gibbs and James Earl Green were murdered at Jackson State, and though a federal grand jury was convened, it was done in the knowledge that no Southern grand jury would be likely to indict a Mississippi law-enforcement officer. Now, at Southern University in Louisiana, it has happened again, and the victims are black. The color of the victims' skin guarantees at least a federal gesture toward justice, something the white victims of Kent State have been denied. But, if past history means anything, it is most unlikely that for Denver Smith and Leonard Brown there will be the kind of justice there might have been had they been murdered by someone *not* in a police or military uniform. And so the lessons to be learned from these brutal killings will go unlearned once more.

Appendices

Appendix I
From *American Report:* Due Process Forbids Soldiers in Civil Disorders

by David E. Engdahl

According to official Pentagon statistics, the National Guard was used to deal with civil disorders on 221 separate occasions between September 1967 and June 1970. During the one month of May 1970, National Guardsmen were activated on twenty-four separate occasions at twenty-one universities in sixteen states. Despite the tragic consequences of their use that fateful month, frequent use of National Guardsmen in civil-disorder situations has continued during the last year and a half.

No sensible citizen is likely to deny that when destructive civil disorder actually occurs there must be some sufficient means in the government to bring it to an end. One might have doubted, however, whether, in a nation which has traditionally served as a refuge from military tyranny abroad, the use of military force against civilians could be an acceptable means. The tragedy of May 4, 1970, has set many Americans to wondering how it is that this practice has become a part of our national life, whether it is consistent with either our law or our traditions, and whether it can be brought to an end. The truth is, it became a part of our practice by default only a century ago, at a time when violence and high passion had impaired both temperance and reason; it is inconsistent both with our traditions and with our contemporary law; but nonetheless it can be brought to an end only by great and concerted effort on the part of those deeply enough committed to the values of life and freedom to really care.

The roots of our law run deep. In the year 1181, Henry II of England ordered every free man in England to keep arms and swear to use them in service of the King. His purpose was twofold: to provide a defense force to supplement the feudal army in the event of foreign attack, and to provide a pursuit force to aid the King's sheriffs in subduing malefactors to be held for civil trial. The same *jurata ad arma*—the citizens sworn to arms—were to fulfill both roles. There was then no real distinction in English law between civil and military affairs.

Over the next two centuries, however, as the common law of England began to take shape, the two functions of the *jurata ad arma* became clearly distinct. As a defense force they were placed under the control of officials peculiarly concerned with military affairs, and when so employed they were subject to what early came to be known as martial or military law. But in their other role they remained under the control of the sheriffs and, like the sheriffs, subject to the very different rules of the developing common law. As a defense force, the *jurata ad arma* developed into the militia; as an aid to the sheriff for purposes of law enforcement, the *jurata ad arma* developed into the *posse comitatus*—"the power of the county"—or simply, the sheriff's posse. The point is that it was precisely the same people—all able-bodied men of age—who composed both the militia and the posse; what distinguished the two forces was the difference in the officials who had them in charge, and the differences in the laws which set limits to what each of the forces, or their members, could do.

These differences became more clear during the fourteenth century. When peasant mobs rioted in England in 1381, the riots were suppressed by the citizens as the posse. However, the posse employed force in a fashion which, while appropriate for a field of war, violated the standards of reason and restraint demanded of sheriffs—and thus of the posse—by the common law. For their overzealousness in enforcement, the members of the posse would have been prosecuted and punished had the King not pardoned them for their offense in suppressing the riots (in the words of the pardon) "without due process of law." It had been settled by Parliament some fifty years before that so long as the institutions of the civilian law had not been shut down, military measures were against the law. Even the King was not permitted to use military force against his subjects, but must treat them according to "due process of law."

Thus no less than six centuries ago the law drew a bold line between war and civil disorder, and between sheer armed force and due process of law. When kings in later years disregarded this distinction, again and again it was reasserted and reclaimed by the people—more often than not, by revolution.

The first English riot act was enacted by Parliament in 1412. It called for suppression of riots by the sheriff, with the aid of the posse. No provision was made for the use of the militia, and it is perfectly clear why: the militia when mustered into service was a military force not bound by due process of law, and riots could be suppressed only in accordance with due process. During the sixteenth century, however, a new type of royal military official was created and employed to suppress civil disorders by military force, superseding the sheriff and posse. By 1627 this practice in derogation of the due-process tradition had built up considerable popular resentment. When King Charles I in that year sent soldiers to quell disorders in several towns, it so outraged the people that the next session of Parliament delayed all its other business and prepared that monumental document of English liberty, the Petition of Right, insisting that military measures taken within the realm were unlawful and demanding that the King respect the law. Charles, however, continued to employ military measures in England until his repeated acts of tyranny precipitated revolution and cost Charles his head.

The principle of the Petition of Right was implemented by Parliament and reemphasized on several occasions during the later seventeenth century. It became firmly settled that, although an armed assault by foreigners or subjects to actually depose the government might be repelled by military force, civil disorders, or riots regardless of their gravity, must never be suppressed by the use of soldiers. A new riot act in 1714 repeated the established rule: riots must be suppressed by civilian officials with the aid of the posse—all of them subject to the restraints of due process. There was no authority for the use of soldiers to suppress any civil disorder, regardless of how aggravated the circumstances might be.

With this background, it is easy to understand the anger of the American colonists when, for several years before they crossed the threshold of revolution, British soldiers were used to suppress civil disorders in the colonies. The tragedy at Boston on March 5, 1770, that became known as the Boston Massacre, was an outrage, not because the unruly mob of Bostonians was doing right, but because for soldiers to be employed against such wrongdoers was a violation of that oldest and most essential principle which generations of Englishmen had struggled to maintain as the primary safeguard of liberty itself. (The soldiers who fired at Boston were indicted and tried, and two at least convicted of manslaughter. What would have been the response of the colonists if there had been, not merely no indictment, but a refusal even to instigate a grand jury investigation?)

A crucial development in the law occurred in England in 1780. A major riot in London, lasting several days, was finally suppressed by the use of soldiers. Afterwards the members of Parliament heatedly debated whether this was not a violation of the principle just discussed. The view which prevailed, and which soon became settled in American as well as English law, was that of Lord Chief Justice Mansfield. Mansfield's doctrine acknowledged that riots were to be suppressed only by civil officers and the posse, and never by military force. He pointed out, however, that the same persons who were members of the army were also members of the posse, which included all able-bodied men of age; and he concluded that, regardless of whether they wore army uniforms or not, they could be called to suppress a riot, "not as soldiers, but as citizens." The critical point was that when employed to suppress a riot they acted in their capacity as members of the civilian posse, and not as soldiers, and were therefore subject to civilian law and command exactly like any other citizen called to aid a sheriff. Only on this view could the use of "soldiers" be reconciled with the historic principle of due process of law.

A careful review of the records of the Constitutional Convention, the ratification debates, the congressional preparation of the Bill of Rights, and the legislation of early Congresses concerning the army and the militia discloses unmistakably that the traditional prohibition of military force in civil disorders, as adapted by Lord Chief Justice Mansfield's doctrine, was understood and deliberately preserved by the statesmen of that period as inherent in the concept of due process of law. The ancient notion of a posse of laymen was much less adapted to the social conditions of the nineteenth century than to those of the thirteenth century; yet nothing resembling the modern civilian police force had yet been established. The Mansfield Doctrine made available a practical source of manpower for law enforcement while preserving the traditional—and now constitutional—prohibition against military force. So the practice of using "soldiers" (selected militiamen or regular army men) *as civilians* for law enforcement continued for two generations. From court opinions as well as other records it is clear that they were regarded, when so used, as civilians under the command of the ordinary civil officials, and bound by the standards of due process of law.

But then came the upheaval of civil war. Soldiers now were heroes for their exploits *as soldiers,* not abroad, but at home. Demands for efficient implementation of the social mandate of victory led to nakedly military techniques of reconstructing the defeated South. Even after reconstruction, troops were frequently called out by federal marshals to intimidate or over-power civil officers as well as private citizens in the South. It was claimed that military intimidation at the polls actually swung the Presidential election of 1876.

Congress moved to end these excesses in 1878; but because the war and reconstruction years had obscured the notion that troops could be used as civilians under civil law, the act of 1878 had disastrous unintended effects. The Mansfield Doctrine as applied earlier in America had meant two things: first, that a sheriff or a marshal could use soldiers as a posse without the chief executive's assent; and second, that whenever used in law-enforcement situations—whether by sheriff or marshal or President—they were civilians subject to civilian command and law.

The second and more critical point had been forgotten in the fury of the war; so, instead of reemphasizing the subordination of such troops to civilian institutions and law, Congress merely prohibited the use of federal troops as a posse. This foreclosed their use by marshals or others than the President himself, but did not negate the statutes authorizing the President to use troops in domestic situations. What it did do, by explicitly forbidding their use *as a posse,* was to reinforce the erroneous notion that when the President did use troops in a civil disorder they could be treated *as soldiers* rather than as civilians. A parallel development occurred in popular under-standing concerning the use of militia, or National Guardsmen, in the states.

The rest is familiar history. The use of soldiers *as soldiers* in civil dis-orders has become a routine practice. What has not, until now, been ap-parent, however, is that this is *precisely* the practice which was forbidden at the very birth of the English common law; which precipitated revolutions in seventeenth-century England; which inflamed the first patriots of the Amer-ican nation; which was early and insistently decried in the chambers of state legislatures and the Congress; and which was sedulously avoided until the Civil War!

Massachusetts is Ohio, and Boston is Kent; March 5, 1770, is May 4, 1970, and the Boston Massacre is "Kent State." Will there be revolution by 1976?

Revolution takes various forms. In England in the seventeenth century it took two revolutions to establish safeguards against military oppression. The first was resisted, and consequently was won only after bitter civil war. The second, however, was led by men who themselves held positions of legiti-mate power in the state; hence it was bloodless, and earned the title the Glorious Revolution. What may be done toward a glorious revolution in these United States?

On one front, litigation is seeking to enforce the same standards of liability under the standards of due process for the acts of soldiers against civilians that would apply to civilian officials. State statutes, unheard of before the Civil War, granting special immunities to soldiers for their violence in civil disorders, must be invalidated or repealed. But this is only the beginning. Perhaps the use of "soldiers" in riots—even their use "as civilians"—should be prohibited altogether. Or if not that, at least steps must be taken to modify their indoctrination and training and their techniques of riot control to make it perfectly and emphatically clear to them and all others that on such duty they are *in no sense* soldiers, or bound by military discipline or orders, but are wholly governed by civilian officers and the restraints of civil law. Legislation, very carefully designed, can do much toward this goal, and is now being urged; but its enactment will depend upon the extent to which citizens apprehend and insist upon the principle that is at stake.

The revolution that is needed is not the espousal of some new, innovative creed, but rather a new attention to the lessons of our history and the fundamental principles of our heritage. It is revolution akin to revival; and like the self-assessment and repentance involved in revival, it may entail reassessment of other practices as well. Seeing how wrong is our use of military force in domestic situations, we may come to question our use of it even abroad. Or perhaps, seeing how utterly repugnant to our deepest traditions is this one current practice, we may be spurred to examine other features of our contemporary polity with the same critical bent of mind.

No effort can undo the tragedy of Kent State; and to seek only retribution for the wrong that was done would be vain. But what a memorial to the victims of that tragedy would be our steady resolve to accomplish the redemption of that fundamental safeguard of liberty, the uncompromising subordination of military power to ordinary civilian authority and law!

Mr. Engdahl is Associate Professor of Law and Director of the Law Revision Center at the University of Colorado School of Law, Boulder, where he has taught Constitutional Law since 1966.

Appendix II
From *American Report:* Kent State: Why the Church?

by Rev. John P. Adams

Why should the church be concerned with events like those which took place at Kent State University and Jackson State College in 1970? That is a question that has been raised repeatedly in recent weeks, especially since one of the denominations involved in the issues arising out of these incidents has been sued. Many persons make the assumption that the killing of students at Kent State and Jackson State is a fact with which only the government should be concerned—that the government at some level, through one agency or another, will appropriately investigate and then give the whole matter proper disposition.

The church, it is maintained, should be busy with the business of "reconciliation" while others are doing the investigating. Yet, surely reconciliation can never require that the facts be glossed over or the truth be hidden. Reconciliation cannot be purchased at the price of injustice. Reconciliation is not a smoothing over and a return to normal. It is, more, advancing in the power of love toward new truth which effects fresh relationships.

Consequently, when various governmental agencies issue varying reports with conflicting testimony about an event in which human life was irresponsibly taken, the church must focus on that as a fact to be dealt with in the process of reconciliation. Otherwise, "getting back to normal," if that is what reconciliation means to some, would require us to believe that it is normal for unarmed students to be killed on their own campuses by armed agents of the government.

The killing at Kent took place at high noon on a bright, sunny spring day. Nearly three thousand photographs, it is said, were taken of the confrontation between the Ohio National Guard and the students at Kent State University on May 4, 1970. On that day, Ohio National Guardsmen, armed with M-1 combat rifles, advanced on an assembly of students which both the Scranton Commission report and the Justice Department summary of the FBI report said was initially peaceful and quiet. Within half an hour of that advance, four students were killed and nine were wounded.

That event is a graphic example—perhaps the clearest and most classic illustration—of the irresponsible and unlawful use of firearms by a government against its own citizens. Such abuses of authority often take place in the United States—in certain cities and in contacts between the police and minority citizens particularly—but they are usually without witnesses and rarely photographed. At Kent State there were hundreds of witnesses, and prize-winning photographs depict the entire event. Consequently, the Kent event must not be allowed to fade into the past until the real truth is known about the shooting and until responsibility for it is determined.

If a state governmental whitewash is allowed to stand as the only expression of justice relating to the killing, then a single, simple signal is sent across the country to all those who have official authority to use firearms in their contact with citizens: "You can fire indiscriminately and kill with impunity." Needless to say, no society which desires to stand and be stable can permit the sanctioning of the abuse of official power.

The Attorney General of the United States, in agreeing with the President's Commission on Campus Unrest, called the shooting at Kent "unnecessary, unwarranted, and inexcusable," and then announced that the case was closed. That cannot be satisfactory, for it furnishes a *warrant* to kill for those who, in their official capacities, decide that it is *necessary* to shoot and who can make up the *excuses* afterward.

Justice Louis Brandeis, who sat on the Supreme Court of the United States from 1916 to 1939, once wrote in an opinion: "Crime is contagious. If the Government becomes a law breaker, it breeds contempt for the law; it invites every man to become a law unto himself; it invites anarchy."

Little has been said about the fact that the few anarchistic acts of youthful protesters have followed so closely those instances of law breaking by the government. In a time in which we are urging young people to renew a faith in the so-called "system," it is absolutely essential that the government demonstrate that justice is not a political tool to protect some and punish others.

The Report of Lawlessness and Law Enforcement, issued by the United States Commission on Law Observance and Enforcement in 1931, stated: "Respect for law, which is the fundamental prerequisite of law observance, hardly can be expected of people in general if the officers charged with enforcement of the law do not set the example of obedience to its precepts."

The 1931 report became emphatic about this effect when it stated: "This official law breaking . . . recalls the story of the Dukhobor who tried to go naked in the streets of London. 'A policeman set out gravely to capture him, but found himself distanced because of his heavy clothing. Therefore, he divested himself, as he ran, of garment after garment until he was naked; and so lightened, he caught his prey. But then it was impossible to tell which was the Dukhobor and which was the policeman.' " When it becomes almost impossible to distinguish between those who break the law and those who have the responsibility for enforcing the law, the church—and all other parts of the society—must be concerned and must be involved in finding the correctives.

It has been suggested that the killing of students in May 1970 was actually effective in quieting the campuses and in restoring order by causing students to return to their books instead of demonstrating their concern for the brutality of the Vietnam War and the injustices to the poor in our own country. Those who believe this point to the "campus calm" during the past year.

In the middle of the condensation of James Michener's book *Kent State: What Happened and Why,* in the April issue of *Reader's Digest,* there was an advertisement for Ortho Chevron Chemical Company. In advertising insecticides for use in gardens, black bold words stated: "The balance of nature is predicated on the fact that one thing dies so that another may live." Some believe that this is what happened. Some believe that the shooting of students at Kent was necessary in order that other students could live and the society could be preserved. Yet no reference is made to the depression and despair, the agony and the anguish, which have been sharply felt by so many students.

The frustration of students, so openly expressed in 1970, has been driven inwards and burns there within. As young people search for ways creatively and constructively to express their concerns, channels must be opened. The "system" now has a heavy burden of proof. It must show that dissent in a democratic society is not dangerous. It must open a process that was closed by bullets in May of 1970.

The lowering of the voting age may have been one way by which a channel was opened, and youth may answer the bullets with ballots. As a result, even though some governmental leaders tried to maintain power "out of the barrel of a gun" (as Mao Tse-tung suggested), the young may balance that power by pulling voting levers and help determine the new leadership of the country. The whole community, including the church, should be concerned with the psychic vacuum that was left in the lives of the young across the nation after May 1970, and must give encouragement and strong support as youth attempt once again to participate in the political process.

Yet it must be understood that the protection of the rights of citizens is not only for the benefit of the young, nor can it be accomplished by them alone. It is for every American citizen of every age. The message is clear. No citizen is safe when certain citizens can be summarily executed. When these rights are taken away by the gun, we have moved a long step toward full governmental repression in our country.

Repression is not something which a government announces as a policy. It is always called something else and comes in small ways. It usually comes in the form of protection for those who are afraid, or as a privilege for those who have position, or the furnishing of something for those who are in need. Yet it must be detected in its incipient form, and when it is discovered, it must be fully resisted. The church has a special responsibility in such a time, for religious faith may be used to bless the repressive acts. But when the church permits the gospel of freedom to become a tool of repression, there is not only unfaithfulness to her Lord; there is also a pious approval given to the destruction of life.

We in this country, in this time, should remember the works of Martin Niemoeller, the German pastor who resisted the Nazis and who was imprisoned for bearing witness. He said, after his liberation from a World War II concentration camp: "We knew the wrong and the right path, but we did not warn the people and allowed them to rush forward to their doom.

I, too, have failed, for I, too, have been silent when I should have spoken." We do not have to draw false comparisons in order to see some similarities. Already many of us have remained silent when we should have spoken, for we have seen others put down when they have spoken. Also, we have heard some citizens speak of the repressive acts of government to which they have been subjected, but since we have not experienced them ourselves, we have assumed that surely these people were exaggerating, or the instances to which they were referring were clear exceptions to what ordinarily takes place.

The church must open its eyes and see what is happening, and perhaps it is really able to see and believe that there is a repressive trend only when it observes it in an event like Kent. If the church cannot see it in such a clear example, then it will hardly recognize such a trend when it is more effectively disguised in the policies and procedures of governmental agencies. If we do not see it, then we may, as a church, finally have to declare to the rest of the world those words which the Council of the Protestant Church in Germany declared in 1945, after World War II: "We accuse ourselves for not witnessing more courageously, for not praying more faithfully, for not believing more joyously, and for not loving more ardently."

Rev. Adams is Director of the Department of Law, Justice, and Community Relations of the Board of Church and Society of the United Methodist Church.

I wish to express here my appreciation to the authors and to Ron Henderson and the editors of *American Report* for their permission to include these two articles from the magazine's special supplement, "Kent State Revisited," published in November 1971.

P.D.

Appendix III
1. Department of Justice Summary of the FBI Investigation: Principal Conclusions

1. Most persons estimate that about 200–300 students were gathered around the Victory Bell on the Commons with another 1,000 or so gathered on the hill directly behind them. Apparently, the crowd was without a definite leader, although at least three persons carried flags.

2. The crowd apparently was initially peaceful and relatively quiet.

3. Information suggests that it was the Ohio National Guard who determined that the rally would not be held.

4. Just prior to the time the Guard left its position on the practice field, members of Troop G were ordered to kneel and aim their weapons at the students in the parking lot south of Prentice Hall. They did so, but did not fire. One person, however, probably an officer, at this point did fire a pistol in the air. No guardsman admits firing this shot.

5. Some guardsmen, including General Canterbury and Major Jones, claim that the Guard did run out of tear gas at this time. However, in fact, it had not.

6. Forty-seven Guardsmen claim they did not fire their weapons. There are substantial indications that at least two and possibly more Guardsmen are lying concerning this fact.

7. The Guardsmen were not surrounded. Regardless of the location of the students following them, photographs and television film show that only a very few students were located between the Guard and the Commons. They could easily have continued in the direction in which they had been going.

8. No guardsman claims he was hit with rocks immediately prior to the shooting.

9. Only one guardsman, Lawrence Shafer, was injured on May 4, 1970, seriously enough to require any kind of medical treatment. He admits his injury was received some 10 to 15 minutes before the fatal volley was fired.

10. One Guardsman specifically states that the quantity of rock throwing was not as great just prior to the shooting as it had been before.

11. There was no sniper.

221

12. The great majority of Guardsmen do not state that they were under sniper fire and many specifically state that the first shots came from the National Guardsmen.

13. At least one person who has not admitted firing his weapon, did so. The FBI is currently in possession of four spent .45 cartridges which came from a weapon not belonging to any person who admitted he fired. The FBI has recently obtained all .45's of persons who claimed they did not fire, and is checking them against the spent cartridges.

14. Sergeant Robert James of Company A assumed he'd been given an order to fire, so he fired once in the air. As soon as he saw some of the men of the 107th (Troop G) were firing into the crowd, he ejected his remaining seven shells so he would not fire any more.

15. Sergeant Rudy Morris of Troop G prepared to fire his weapon but stopped when he realized that the "rounds were not being placed."

16. Sergeant Richard Love of Company C fired once in the air, then saw others firing into the crowd; he asserted he "could not believe" that the others were shooting into the crowd, so he lowered his weapon.

17. There was no request from any Guardsman for permission to fire his weapon. Some Guardsmen, including some who claimed their lives were in danger and some who fired their weapons, had their backs to the students when the firing broke out.

18. Four students were killed, nine others wounded, three seriously. Of the students who were killed, Jeff Miller's body was found 85–90 yards from the Guard. Allison Krause fell about 100 yards away. William Schroeder and Sandy Scheuer were approximately 130 yards away from the Guard when they were shot.

19. Although both Miller and Krause had probably been in the front ranks of the demonstrators initially, neither was in a position to pose even a remote danger to the National Guard at the time of the firing. Sandy Scheuer, as best as we can determine, was on her way to a speech therapy class. We do not know whether Schroeder participated in any way in the confrontation that day.

20. Of the 13 Kent State students shot, none, so far as we know, were associated with either the disruption in Kent on Friday night, May 1, 1970, or the burning of the ROTC building on Saturday, May 2, 1970.

21. Aside entirely from any questions of specific intent on the part of the Guardsmen or a predisposition to use their weapons, we do not know what started the shooting. We can only speculate on the possibilities. For example, Sergeant Leon Smith of Company A stated that he saw a man about 20 feet from him running at him with a rock. Sergeant Smith then says he fired his shotgun once in the air. He alone of all the Guardsmen does not mention hearing shooting prior to the time he fired . . . It is also possible that the members of Troop G observed their top noncommissioned officer, Sergeant Pryor, turn and point his weapon at the crowd and followed his example. Sergeant Pryor admits that he was pointing his weapon at the students prior to the shooting but claims he was loading it and denies he fired. The FBI does not be-

lieve he fired. Another possibility is that one of the Guards either panicked and fired first, or intentionally shot at a student, thereby triggering the other shots.

22. We have some reason to believe that the claim by the National Guard that their lives were endangered by the students was fabricated subsequent to the event.

2. Attorney General Mitchell's Statement

FOR IMMEDIATE RELEASE
FRIDAY, AUGUST 13, 1971

Attorney General John N. Mitchell issued the following statement today:

The Department of Justice has completed its analysis and evaluation of all the available facts and information surrounding the tragic deaths of four Kent State University students on May 4, 1970.

Immediately after the incident occurred, I requested the Civil Rights Division and the Federal Bureau of Investigation to make a careful, thorough and intensive investigation, which continued through the summer. Hundreds of persons were interviewed, including students, National Guardsmen, school officials, and townspeople. Reports totaling approximately 8,000 pages were submitted.

As the investigation was drawing to a close, the State of Ohio proposed to convene a special grand jury. In accordance with our policy of deferring to local action, we extended our cooperation to state officials and made copies of the complete FBI investigation available to the Attorney General of Ohio. We also made copies of it available to the President's Commission on Campus Unrest.

When the Ohio special grand jury made its report public on October 16, 1970, the Department of Justice resumed and intensified its evaluation of the entire matter, including the reports of the state grand jury and the Commission.

All of this information has been thoroughly analyzed by Department attorneys to determine whether there existed any violations of federal laws. Subsequently, I received a recommendation from the Civil Rights Division. In addition, I have personally reviewed the case.

The facts available to me support the conclusion reached by the President's Commission that the rifle fire was, in the words of the Commission, "unnecessary, unwarranted and inexcusable." However, our review persuades me that there is no credible evidence of a conspiracy between National Guardsmen to shoot students on the campus and that there is no likelihood of successful prosecutions of individual guardsmen.

It is my judgment that further action by the Department of Justice would not be warranted. In view of the massive federal investigative resources already committed, and the intensive examination of the results of the investigations, it appears clear that further investigation by a federal grand jury could not reasonably be expected to produce any new evidence which would contribute further to making a prosecutive judgment.

A sense of tragedy over the events which took place at Kent is as common to everyone in the Department as it is to the American people, but this incident cannot be undone. I am satisfied that the Department has taken every possible action to serve justice.

I have communicated this decision to the parents of the four students who died and restated my sympathy with the full knowledge that nothing can be said to mitigate their remorse and sorrow. We can only hope that any type of recurrence can be avoided by this experience and that incidents like this will never again be a part of our national life.

Appendix IV
The Ohio National Guard
at Kent State

A few days after the first anniversary of the killings at Kent State, attorneys for Generals Del Corso and Canterbury returned to Steven Sindell the interrogatory he had submitted to them in connection with Arthur Krause's suit. Although several questions put to the generals went unanswered—the Fifth Amendment was invoked—a roster of all Ohio National Guardsmen activated for duty on May 4, 1970, was furnished to Sindell, along with a list of the guardsmen who had fired their weapons.

Attorney Sindell had asked for the name, rank, and address of every guardsman involved in the shooting, but, as he had anticipated, the generals refused to supply the information, citing the Fifth Amendment. Several questions later, however, in answer to a rather innocuous question, the generals said simply, "Refer to Exhibit 3," which, it turned out, was a list of names captioned: "Prior Service and Riot Duty Training of Individuals Who Fired Weapons."

All the guardsmen identified by the Justice Department as having fired on May 4, 1970, were listed, with the exception of five men: Leon Smith and William Herschler (Company A); Richard Love and Richard Lutey (Company C), and Lawrence Shafer of Troop G. Herschler has denied firing and therefore was not surprisingly omitted from the Guard list, but the absence of Smith, who admitted to the FBI that he fired one round from his shotgun into the air, may be the result of a clerical error or may indicate that he did not meet the requirements of the caption's proviso on riot-duty training. Love and Lutey both admitted to the FBI that they fired; so their absence from the Guard list might be explained by the fact that Company C was not officially at the Pagoda. Why Shafer was not included in the list is a mystery. We know, from the Justice Department, that he had served in the Guard for four and a half years, had sixty hours of riot-control training, and had been activated for riot duty on three previous occasions. Furthermore, he admitted to the FBI that he had fired one round at a student, later identified as Joseph Lewis, and four rounds in the air.

Exhibit 3 gave the names and ranks of twenty-four Ohio National Guardsmen. The Justice Department stated that a "minimum" of twenty-nine fired their weapons. We know, by their own admission, that Smith, Love, Lutey, and Shafer fired, and we know that the Justice Department believes that Herschler fired. The addition of these five guardsmen accords the figure of twenty-nine, but there remains the allegation by the Justice Department that at least two guardsmen were lying when they claimed they did not fire their weapons. Assuming Herschler is one of the two, who is the other? The Justice Department reported that seven members of Troop G admitted firing, but not at the students, and five admitted "firing a total of eight shots into the crowd or at a specific student," for a total of twelve men in Troop G. The Ohio National Guard list has ten names, and even adding Sergeant Shafer, we are one man short. Who is the unidentified twelfth member of Troop G who the FBI found had fired his gun? The Justice Department implies it was not Sergeant Myron C. Pryor by stating that the FBI "does not believe he fired." If not Pryor, then who?

As for the rest of the interrogatory, the answers given by General Canterbury to certain questions concerning Allison Krause bear inclusion here if only to emphasize the extent to which the Ohio National Guard was prepared to go in its determination to frustrate justice and shift responsibility for the killings onto the victims. The questions put to General Canterbury were carefully phrased, so as to make it almost impossible for anyone to misunderstand their meaning:

Q. Do you claim that Allison Krause in any manner caused any injury whatsoever to any member of the Ohio National Guard who fired a weapon immediately prior to or at the time of the shooting?

A. Yes.

Q. If your answer is in the affirmative, then state with specificity and in detail the factual basis for any and all reasons for such claim, including the names and addresses of any and all persons who may have knowledge supporting such claim.

A. Allison Krause was unknown to me, so that it is unknown whether she was one of those rioters who caused injury to members of the National Guard immediately prior to the shooting.

Such flatly contradictory statements in a court procedure speak for themselves; they are only too typical of the excuses and explanations that were given out by the Ohio National Guard during the weeks following the shootings at Kent State.

Exhibit 3, and the roster of guardsmen activated for duty, indicates that the following members of the Ohio National Guard were at the Pagoda at the time of the shooting. Those identified as having fired include guardsmen who admitted doing so to the FBI. Claims of injury were reported by the Ohio National Guard. With respect to Troop G, we know that one, possibly more, of the seven men listed as not having fired did in fact fire.

RANK	NAMES	UNIT	FIRED	CLAIMS INJURY
BG	CANTERBURY, Robert H.	HHD/OARNG	No	No
1LT	TUCKER, Ralph G.	CO.H/107th	No	No
CPT	SRP, Raymond J.	Troop G	No	No
2LT	STEVENSON, Alexander D.	"	No	No
1SG	PRYOR, Myron C.	"	No	Yes
SFC	FLESHER, Okey R.	"	Yes	Yes
SSG	MORRIS, Barry W.	"	Yes	Yes
SSG	MORRIS, Rudy E.	"	No	No
SGT	BRECKENRIDGE, Dennis L.	"	Yes	No
SGT	SHAFER, Lawrence A.	"	Yes	Yes
SGT	SHOLL, Joseph D.	"	Yes	Yes
SP5	CASE, William J.	"	Yes	Yes
SP4	BACLAWSKI, John R.	"	No	Yes
SP4	McGEE, James D.	"	Yes	Yes
SP4	PERKINS, William E.	"	Yes	Yes
SP4	PIERCE, James E.	"	Yes	Yes
SP4	THOMAS, Lloyd W.	"	Yes	Yes
SP4	ZOLLER, Ralph W.	"	Yes	Yes
PFC	McCOY, Michael D.	"	No	No
PFC	McCOY, Paul R.	"	No	Yes
CPT	MARTIN, John E.	Company A	No	No
1LT	KLINE, Dwight G.	"	No	No
2LT	FALLON, Howard R.	"	No	No
SGT	McMANUS, Mathew J.	"	Yes	Yes
SGT	WENTSCH, William G.	"	No	No
SP5	BIXLER, David A.	"	No	No
SP5	BRAGG, Bruce W.	"	No	No
SP5	FRISCH, John A.	"	No	No
SP5	MAAS, Roger A.	"	Yes	Yes
SP5	McQUATE, Raymond D.	"	No	No
SP5	MICHALAK, Daniel C.	"	No	No
SP5	SNURE, David L.	"	No	No
SP4	ANTRAM, Dale L.	"	No	No
SP4	BRACHNA, Gabor S.	"	No	No
SP4	CORNELIUS, Gary A.	"	No	No
SP4	CRATER, James R.	"	No	No
SP4	CRILOW, Keith E.	"	No	No
SP4	EMCH, Erich R.	"	No	No
SP4	FARRISS, James W.	"	Yes	Yes
SP4	HERSCHLER, William F.	"	?	No
SP4	JAMES, Robert D.	"	Yes	Yes
SP4	KLINGERMAN, Dean H.	"	No	No
SP4	MAST, Ted W.	"	No	No
SP4	MILETTO, Carl A.	"	No	No
SP4	MOORHEAD, Robert P.	"	No	No
SP4	MORRIS, Robert K.	"	No	No

RANK	NAMES	UNIT	FIRED	CLAIMS INJURY
SP4	MOSER, Dewey E.	Company A	No	No
SP4	MYERS, Ronnie B.	"	Yes	No
SP4	REPP, Russell E., Jr.	"	Yes	Yes
SP4	ROGERS, David E.	"	No	No
SP4	SMITH, Leon H.	"	Yes	No
SP4	TAGGART, Wayne R.	"	No	No
SP4	ZIMMERMAN, Paul R.	"	No	Yes
PFC	BIDDLE, Rodney R.	"	Yes	No
PFC	BOSS, Steven L.	"	No	No
PFC	BROWN, James K.	"	Yes	Yes
PFC	BURGER, Albert L., Jr.	"	No	No
PFC	FARRISS, Thomas O.	"	No	No
PFC	GAMMELL, Ronald D.	"	No	No
PFC	HUFF, Norman L.	"	No	No
PFC	JONES, Jeffrey L.	"	No	No
PFC	LORENTZ, Richard A.	"	No	No
PFC	MILLER, Stephen J.	"	No	No
PFC	MOWRER, Larry R.	"	Yes	No
PFC	NAUJOKS, Paul R.	"	No	No
PFC	RABER, Phillip D.	"	Yes	Yes
PFC	SHADE, Richard R.	"	Yes	Yes
PFC	SNYDER, Richard B.	"	Yes	Yes
PFC	STANFORD, Richard D.	"	No	No
PV2	BOYES, Roy V.	"	No	No
PV2	HATFIELD, Robert D.	"	Yes	No
PV2	HINTON, Lonnie D.	"	Yes	No
SGT	LOVE, Richard K.	Company C	Yes	No
SP4	LUTEY, Richard	"	Yes	No
MAJ	JONES, Harry D.	HHC/145th	No	No
LTC	FASSINGER, Charles E.	HHT/2/107th	No	No

Bibliography

Official reports

Department of Justice Summary of the FBI Investigation, 1970. Reprinted in I. F. Stone: *The Killings at Kent State: How Murder Went Unpunished.*

Franklin, Doris, Kathy L. Stafford, Kathleen Whitmer, and Jeffrey E. Zink: *Kent State University Commission on May 1–4 Violence: Minority Report.* 1971.

Presidential Commissions. Hearings before the Subcommittee on Administrative Practice and Procedure of the Committee on the Judiciary, U.S. Senate. Washington, D.C.: Government Printing Office, 1971.

The President's Commission on Campus Unrest. Washington, D.C.: U.S. Government Printing Office, 1970.

Books and pamphlets

Ahern, James F.: *Police in Trouble.* New York: Hawthorn Books, 1972.

Casale, Ottavio M. and Louis Paskoff: *The Kent Affair: Documents and Interpretations.* Boston: Houghton Mifflin, 1971.

Committee for Truth and Justice at Kent State University: *Report of the Kent State Grand Jury.* This unofficial inquiry is the only existing "grand jury" investigation into the circumstances surrounding the killing of the four students.

Cronkite, Walter: *Eye on the World.* New York: Cowles, 1971.

Davies, Peter and The Board of Church and Society of the United Methodist Church: *An Appeal for Justice.* Congressional Record, July 22, 1971.

Engdahl, David E.: *Soldiers, Riots, and Revolution: The Law and History of Military Troops in Civil Disorders.* The Law Revision Center, University of Colorado, July 1971.

Eszterhas, Joe and Michael D. Roberts: *13 Seconds: Confrontation at Kent State.* New York: Dodd, Mead, 1970.

Michener, James A.: *Kent State: What Happened and Why.* New York: Random House, and Reader's Digest Press, 1971.

Nelson, Jack and Jack Bass: *The Orangeburg Massacre.* New York: World, 1970.

Reporting the Kent State Incident. New York: American Newspaper Publishers Association Foundation, January 1971.

Salisbury, Harrison E., ed.: *The Eloquence of Protest: Voices of the 70's.* Boston: Houghton Mifflin, 1972.

Stone, I. F.: *The Killings at Kent State: How Murder Went Unpunished.* New York: A New York Review Book (Vintage Books), 1970.

Tompkins, Phillip K. and Elaine Vanden Bout Anderson: *Communication Crisis at Kent State: A Case Study.* New York: Gordon & Breach, 1971.

Magazine & newspaper articles

"Conspiracy Charged in Kent Killings: Special Report," *The Pittsburgh Forum,* 1, 39 (July 30, 1971).

Davies, Peter: "Citizens Battle for Justice," *The Nation,* November 29, 1971.

Eszterhas, Joe and Michael D. Roberts: "James Michener's Kent State: A Study in Distortion," *The Progressive,* 35, 9 (September 1971).

Eszterhas, Joe: "Ohio Honors Its Dead," *Rolling Stone,* No. 84 (June 10, 1971).

Hill, Jim Dan (Maj. Gen., ret.): "The Guard at Kent University," *The National Guardsman,* February 1971.

"Kent State Revisited: An Appeal for Justice," *American Report,* November 12, 1971.

"Kent State: The Search for Understanding," Akron *Beacon Journal,* and Knight Newspapers, May 24, 1970.

Lewis, Jerry M.: "A Study of the Kent State Incident Using Smelser's Theory of Collective Behavior," *Sociological Inquiry Journal,* Spring 1972.

Segal, Erich: "Death Story," *Ladies' Home Journal,* October 1970.

Documentary films

"Part of the Family." Produced and directed by Paul Ronder of Summer Morning Films, New York, 1971. National Educational Television, in association with Belafonte Enterprises.

"Kent State: May, 1970." Produced and directed by Alva I. Cox, Jr., of Synesthetics Inc., Washington, D.C., in association with Joseph E. Clement. Narration by E. G. Marshall. September 1972.

Poetry and music

Brubeck, Dave: "Truth Is Fallen." Cincinnati Symphony and Chorus, conducted by Erich Kunzel. Atlantic Recording Corp. 1972.

Davies, Peter: "Requiem for Allison." Poem set to music by Vally Weigl for mezzo or soprano and string quartet. 1971.

White, Claude: "Oh, Broken Flowers (Requiem-Fragments)." University of Pennsylvania Department of Music. December 1970.

Yevtushenko, Yevgeny: *Stolen Apples.* New York: Doubleday & Co., 1971.

Acknowledgments

I wish to thank in particular the parents of Allison, Sandy, and Bill; Attorney Joseph Kelner for his help on behalf of Jeff's mother; John P. Adams and his indispensable staff of two, Carolyn Ross and Clo Winkler; Barry Levine; and Bill Gordon. The support and encouragement of these friends has meant more to me than I can adequately convey in words.

So many people have contributed in different ways to making the book possible, and my appreciation is best expressed in this realization of making our efforts known to the American people. I am especially grateful to Paul Keane, Greg Rambo, Phyllis Curott, Adele Jones, Mrs. Karl Weigl, Steve Sindell, and Paul Rooney.

To the students who assisted me: Bob Dowding, Mark Harris, Bob Huie, Barry Leven, Robert Peabody, Howard Ruffner, Sharon Salyer, Joann Schulte, Debbie Shryock, and Mike White. To those in the news media and publishing field who extended their support: Rona Cherry, Neil Conan, Walter Cronkite, Richard Cooper, George Dawson, Pat Engelhart, Stephen Faye, Paul Fargis, Robert H. Giles, Bill Hershey, David Hess, Harriet Van Horne, John Kifner, Mary McGrory, Daniel Moses, Beverly Pearlman, Merle Pollis, James Ricci, Carl Rowan, Trudy Rubin, Jeff Sallot, Robert Schakne, Beth Sterling, Carl Stern, Sandy Vanocur, Dan Walker, James Wechsler, and Sylvia Wright.

To those in the religious, academic, and political communities who have publicly voiced their concern: Dr. Dean Kelley, Father Robert Chapman, Carolyn Wilhelm, Dr. Dudley Ward, Dr. Grover Bagby, Bishop John H. Burt, Rabbi Richard Hirsch, David Gilman, Bob Jones, Prof. David E. Engdahl, Dr. M. J. Lunine, Prof. Jerry Lewis, Congressmen William Moorhead and Charles A. Vanik, Senators Edward M. Kennedy, George S. McGovern, Robert Taft, Jr., Richard Schweiker, and Edmund Muskie. I am also grateful for the assistance rendered by Bill Maloni of Mr. Moorhead's office and by Senator Kennedy's aides, Mike Epstein and Jim Flug.

I am particularly indebted to Ron Henderson of *American Report;* Robert Shea of *Playboy;* Thomas Hennessy, publisher of the Pittsburgh *Forum;* Harrison Salisbury and David Schneiderman of *The New York*

231

Times; I. F. Stone of the *New York Review of Books;* Tim Coder, Michael Delaney, Reece Morehead, and Mike Levine of Westinghouse Broadcasting. I also thank Al Cox, Joseph E. Clement, and E. G. Marshall for their admirable documentary entitled "Kent State: May, 1970"; Paul Ronder for his film "Part of the Family"; and Bill Moyers for his recent PBS "Journal" episode devoted to reviewing this quest for justice.

On behalf of the parents I express their deep appreciation to those members of the President's Commission on Campus Unrest who publicly called for a federal grand jury investigation: Chairman William Scranton, James F. Ahern, Wm. Matthew Byrne, Jr., Erwin D. Canham, and Joseph Rhodes, Jr.

To those whose names I have failed to mention, excuse my oversight and be assured that your contribution and support are very much appreciated. Through this unique experience I came to meet many persons whom it would not have been possible for me to meet except, perhaps, by chance. I therefore especially appreciate the moments spent with former U.S. Attorney General Ramsey Clark, former Senator Stephen M. Young of Ohio, and I. F. Stone.

As this is the first time I have attempted to write a book, I wish to thank Henry Robbins and Carmen Gomezplata of Farrar, Straus and Giroux, for their patience, advice, and professional guidance. I owe a great debt to both of them. Finally, may I express my love and a very inadequate thank you to my wife, Dorothy, and our three young sons, Steven, John, and Richard. They all had to endure so much more than just the writing of this book.

P.D.

Notes

Introduction

PAGE

3   David Frost Program, May 7, 1970. Metromedia Television.

4   Del Corso's conflicting statements to reporters, from Joe Eszterhas and Michael D. Roberts, *13 Seconds: Confrontation at Kent State* (New York: Dodd, Mead, 1970), p. 280.

5   "Flowers are better than bullets" The myth that Allison had placed the flower in the M-1 was, surprisingly, perpetuated by James Michener in his book on Kent State.

9   Section 242 of the U.S. Code, Title 18: "Whoever under color of any law, statute, ordinance, regulation, or custom willfully subjects any inhabitant . . . to the deprivation of any rights, privileges, or immunities secured or protected by the Constitution of laws of the United States, or to different punishments, pains, or penalties, on account of such inhabitant being an alien, or by reason of his color, or race, than are prescribed for the punishment of citizens, shall be fined etc. . . ."

9   "only question" James F. Ahern, *Police in Trouble* (New York: Hawthorn Books, 1972).

10   "We know almost exactly" James A. Michener, *Kent State: What Happened and Why* (New York: Random House, 1971), p. 543.

Prelude to Violence

13   "when a motorcycle gang" Phillip K. Tompkins and Elaine Anderson, *Communication Crisis at Kent State* (New York: Gordon & Breach, 1971), pp. 10–11.

13   "Many inside the bars" Eszterhas and Roberts, p. 35.

13   "Some of the 'Chosen Few'" Ibid., p. 36.

14   "SDS students had taken over" *The Report of the President's Commission on Campus Unrest* (Washington, D.C.: Government Printing Office, 1970), p. 242. (Hereinafter called the Scranton Commission.)

15   "First, the university police would be" Eszterhas and Roberts, pp. 73–74.

15   "the largest and best-equipped" Tompkins and Anderson, *Communication Crisis at Kent State,* p. 11.

16   "Weathermen had been observed on campus" Eszterhas and Roberts, pp. 74–75.

16   "We were a driverless car" Tompkins and Anderson, p. 16.

16   "they had sufficient manpower" Ibid., p. 22.

16   "for duty only in Kent" Scranton Commission, p. 247.

16   "The group appeared to be" Ibid., p. 247.

16   "unless arrests were necessary . . . at that time" Ibid., pp. 247–48.

17   "it looked as if" Eszterhas and Roberts, p. 76.

17   "substantial cadre of hard-core" Michener, p. 191.

17   "Get it" . . . "Burn it" Scranton Commission, p. 248.

17   "someone burned a miniature American flag" Scranton Commission, p. 248.

17   "an American flag was burned" Justice Department summary of the FBI investigation, 1970, p. 6. (Hereinafter referred to as Justice Department Summary.)

17   "unfurled an American flag" Eszterhas and Roberts, p. 79.

17   "At 8:26 P.M. a young man who" Michener, p. 193.

18   "a significant proportion were not" Tompkins and Anderson, p. 25.

18   "did not begin to burn until 8:45 P.M." Ibid., p. 24.

18   "the fire at ROTC was well ablaze" Michener, p. 195.

18   "the firemen left the ROTC" Justice Department Summary, p. 7.

18   "the building was merely smoldering . . . flame at many points" Michener, p. 197.

18   "the Guard is moving into Kent" Eszterhas and Roberts, p. 82.

18   "a terse command to his troops" Michener, p. 198.

18–19   "cut in the mouth by glass" Scranton Commission, p. 250.

19   "A 21-year-old senior suffered" Eszterhas and Roberts, p. 85.

19   "sweating and angry, bent down" Ibid., p. 85.

19   "identified 13 persons involved" Justice Department Summary, p. 8.

20   "abominable blunder . . . in riot control" *American Report,* April 28, 1972, p. 7.

20   "I'm going to try and close" Eszterhas and Roberts, p. 109.

21   "that Rhodes was two days away" Eszterhas, "Ohio Honors Its Dead," *Rolling Stone,* No. 84 (June 10, 1971), pp. 15–16.

21   "Jim Rhodes changed completely" Michener, p. 250.

21   "last chance to make points" Ibid., p. 251.

21   "The scene here that the city of Kent" Transcription from tape recording distributed by Chestnut Burr, Kent State Year Book, 1971.

22   "As the Ohio law says" Eszterhas and Roberts, pp. 111–12.

22   "no one is safe in Portage County" Ibid., p. 112.

22   "one of the coolest heads on the faculty" Michener, p. 253.

22   "four heavy psychological blows" Ibid., p. 253.

22   "If the President thinks I'm a bum" Ibid., pp. 253–54.

22   "the flamboyant tradition" Ibid., p. 295.

23   "What a lovely day it was" Ibid., p. 255.

24   "the Ohio National Guard was called solely" I. F. Stone, *The Killings at Kent State* (New York: A New York Review Book, 1970), p. 149.

24   "received the impression" Tompkins and Anderson, p. 30.

24   "the Governor's imposition of" Ibid., p. 30.

24   "The Governor, through the National Guard"   Ibid., pp. 30–31.

24–5   "ask for an injunction . . . state of emergency"   Ibid., p. 30.

25   "no official record"   Scranton Commission, p. 255.

25   "not known what person(s)"   Justice Department Summary, p. 9.

25   "providing written authorization"   Scranton Commission, p. 286.

25   "Many students remained confused"   Ibid., p. 256.

25   "Events have taken decisions out of our hands"   Tompkins and Anderson, p. 31.

25   "included a group of coeds"   Scranton Commission, p. 256.

26   "be cancelled and an immediate curfew imposed"   Ibid., p. 256.

26   "rejected the idea . . . negotiating in the streets"   Ibid., p. 257.

26   "The students, previously nonviolent"   Ibid., pp. 257–58.

26   "at least two and probably seven . . . other incidents"   Michener, p. 277.

27   "Many people started running"   Minority Report of the Kent State University Commission on Violence of May 1970, released February 1971, pp. 125–26. Witness #243A. (Hereinafter referred to as the Kent State Commission.)

27   "decided to stay home and study"   Michener, p. 285.

28   "fleeing Kent State students"   Scranton Commission, p. 258.

What Happened on May 4

30   "had just lined up"   Scranton Commission, p. 259.

31   "his desire to withdraw . . . situation persisted"   Tompkins and Anderson, pp. 35–36.

31   "General Canterbury asked"   Ibid., p. 37.

31   "allowed university officials"   Ibid., p. 37.

32   "some had vaguely heard"   Scranton Commission, p. 261.

32   "the validity of subsequent"   Michener, p. 344.

32   "was certainly not illegal in civil law"   Ibid., p. 344.

32   "was acting solely on the"   Ibid., p. 344.

33   "Attention! This is an order"   Ibid., p. 328.

33   "were legitimately in the area"   Scranton Commission, p. 288.

33   "Only when the Guard"   Ibid., p. 288.

33   "none appear to have struck"   Michener, p. 329.

33   "You must not march against the students"   Ibid., p. 331.

33   "These students are going to have to"   Ibid., p. 331.

34   "The May 4 rally began as a peaceful"   Scranton Commission, p. 288.

34   "if any firing was to be done"   Justice Department Summary, p. 16.

34   "it is not known"   Ibid., p. 16.

34   "the distances between the mass of students"   Michener, p. 336.

36   "only one guardsman, Lawrence Shafer, was injured"   Justice Department Summary, p. 25.

36   "His arm, which was badly bruised"   Ibid., p. 25.

36   "especially when launched by coeds . . . weekend warriors, fascists"   Michener, p. 336.

37   "an unknown, but probably substantial"   Justice Department Summary, p. 28.

37   "None are novices"   Ibid., p. 28.

37   "a bushy-haired young man"   Michener, p. 332.

37   "spun around and brought his baton"   Ibid., p. 332.

37   "reached in his pocket"   Ibid., p. 332.

38   "It was inconceivable that soldiers"   Ibid., p. 337.

38   the "Guard's decision to march"   Scranton Commission, p. 288.

38   "walked through the crowd"   Justice Department Summary, p. 19.

38   "elbowing his way through the crowd of students"   Michener, p. 338.

39   "were ordered to kneel and aim"   Justice Department Summary, p. 19.

40   "it appears that they must have"   Michener, p. 339.

40   "if a further command had been given"   Ibid., p. 339.

40   "I happened to have this one Guard"   Ibid., p. 359.

40   "number of rock throwers"   Justice Department Summary, p. 18.

40   "that the rock throwing . . . hit with rocks at this time"   Justice Department Summary, p. 18.

40   "on the parking lot was unruly"   Scranton Commission, p. 267.

40   "It's true that a few kids"   Michener, p. 356.

40   "about fifteen students throw rocks"   Eszterhas and Roberts, p. 157.

40   "twenty-five to thirty people"   Ibid., p. 158.

41   "When the Guard went into their huddle . . . to be interrogated"   Michener, p. 361.

41–2   "It was an accident . . . but not murder"   Ibid., p. 410.

42   "some kind of rough verbal agreement . . . on the practice field"   Ibid., pp. 409–10.

45   Six of the witnesses: Cupp, Howell, Redkey, Onshot, Schott, Tusing   Kent State Commission, pp. 241, 238, 237.

45   "that sudden and dramatic turn"   Michener, p. 409.

46   "one of the guardsmen turned"   Eszterhas and Roberts, pp. 161–62.

47   "that the members of Troop G"   Justice Department Summary, p. 35.

47   "Sergeant Pryor admits that"   Ibid., p. 35.

47   "The FBI does not believe he fired"   Ibid., p. 35.

47   "at least two and possibly more"   Ibid., p. 21.

47   "his entire clip of eight rounds"   Ibid., p. 29.

47   "In addition to Herschler"   Ibid., p. 31.

47   "two men fired pistols"   Scranton Commission, p. 274.

48   "saw one soldier from Company A"   Justice Department Summary, p. 30.

48   "As the troop formation reached"   Scranton Commission, p. 270.

48   "also testified that the closest"   Ibid., 270.

48   "In the direction the Guard fired"   Ibid., p. 270.

50   "SP/4 James Pierce, a Kent State student"   Justice Department Summary, p. 30.

50   "the crowd advanced to within 30 feet"   Ibid., p. 30.

50   "advancing on him . . . had nothing in his hands"   Ibid., p. 30.

50–1   "Six Guardsmen, including two sergeants"   Ibid., pp. 21, 31.

51   "Q. Now with respect to the"   Transcript of testimony before the Scranton Commission.

55   "One official who was responsible"   Michener, p. 368.

58   "Michael Stein, watching from Blanket Hill"   Eszterhas and Roberts, p. 167.

58   "eight shots into the crowd"   Justice Department Summary, p. 30.

Reaction and Inaction

PAGE

140   "nearly 400 bullets"   Scranton Commission, p. 432.

140   "buckshot, rifle slugs, a submachine gun"   Ibid., p. 434.

141   "Call that security guard out there"   Ibid., p. 423.

141   "he did not know how many times"   Ibid., p. 432.

141   of the four hundred Kent State students . . . Michener, p. 453.

142   "Intelligence sources have been reporting"   Ottavio M. Casale and Louis Paskoff, *The Kent Affair* (Boston: Houghton Mifflin, 1971), pp. 68–69.

142   "Although there has been speculation"   Justice Department Summary, pp. 1–2.

145   "refuse to comply with the order"   Scranton Commission, p. 537.

145   "no testimony or other . . . with the order"   Ibid., p. 537.

146   "the most important aspect"   Ibid., p. 231.

147   "Only the magnitude"   Ibid., p. 287.

147   "general issuance of loaded weapons . . . for lethal force"   Ibid., p. 289.

155   "Those who acted . . . had they not done so"   Stone, pp. 148–49.

155   "subject to criminal prosecution"   Ibid., p. 149.

156   "a constant barrage of rocks . . . ranks of the Guardsmen"   Ibid., p. 150.

156   "We call upon our public authorities"   Ibid., p. 152.

156   "The major responsibility"   Ibid., p. 153.

156   "to fix the sole blame"   Ibid., p. 153.

156   "It should be added"   Ibid., p. 150.

157   "should have shot all" . . . There was "no question"   Akron *Beacon Journal,* Oct. 24, 1970.

157   "Communist-inspired" . . . "shoot to kill"   Ibid.

158   "well received among the general public . . . all major universities in America"   Robert O'Neil and Associates, *No Heroes, No Villains* (San Francisco: Jossey-Bass, Inc., 1972), p. 130.

159   "were trying to prove it"   Akron *Beacon Journal,* Nov. 10, 1970.

160   "ended when National Guard troops"   Ibid., Dec. 10, 1970.

160   "Enough has been written about Kent"   Ibid.

161   "What happened in Kent last May"   Akron *Beacon Journal.*

171   "Jeffrey G. Miller and Allison B. Krause"   *The National Guardsman,* Feb. 1971, p. 12.

172   "the FBI has conducted an intensive search"   Justice Department Summary, p. 26.

172   "Frank E. Mianowski, who witnessed"   Akron *Beacon Journal,* May 24, 1970.

172   "definitely could have"   Scranton Commission, p. 281.

184   "free-lance photographer was taking"   Scranton Commission, pp. 279–80.

185   "a student in a sport coat . . . bullets in the chamber"   Eszterhas and Roberts, p. 169.

185   "I was up on the hill after the shooting"   Ibid., pp. 169–70.

185   "rumored to have been hired by the FBI"   Michener, p. 387.

185   "retrieved within minutes"   Ibid., p. 388.

188   "There were 75 Guards present"   Ibid., p. 338.

188   "Alpha Company comprised some 40 to 50 men"   Scranton Commission, p. 263.

188   "I think we could have done a better job"   CBS-TV News, Nov. 3, 1970.

189   "the youth's unhesitating answer"   *Times Picayune*, New Orleans, Sept. 12, 1971.

193   "acting under color of law"   Ibid., p. 183.

194   "There is a wealth of evidence"   Ahern.

194   "Behavior of this kind"   Ibid.

196   "there were unanswered questions"   Jack Nelson and Jack Bass, *The Orangeburg Massacre* (New York: World, 1970), pp. 178–79.

196   "that the probabilities of a conviction"   Ibid., p. 179.

197   "felt the Department had"   Ibid., p. 183.

197   "only brought cases in which"   Ibid., p. 183.

197   "argued that repeated shooting"   Ibid., p. 219.

204   "Perhaps the best way to judge"   Richard Harris, *Justice: The Crisis of Law, Order and Freedom in America* (New York: Avon Books, 1970), pp. 240–41.

Index